21st Century Selling

AN ANTHOLOGY OF ADVICE FROM TOP SALES PROS

Jo Ellynn,

Great meeting you

Good luck !

Joe

JOE
CULLINANE

21st
CENTURY
SELLING

Saratoga, CA

Cullinane, Joe.
    21st century selling: an anthology of advice from top sales pros /
Joe Cullinane and contributors. -- Saratoga, CA : Telum Group, 2002.

        p.   cm.
    ISBN 0-9722495-0-8

    1. Selling.   2. Sales promotion.   I. Title.

HF5438.25 .C85   2002   2002109642
658.85--dc21   0209

Dedication

To Marianne, Charlie and Tina Cullinane.
Thanks for your love and support.

Joe

Contents

PART I – WELCOME TO THE 21ST CENTURY

CHAPTER ONE

CHAPTER TWO

CHAPTER THREE

CHAPTER FOUR

PART II – 21ST CENTURY SELLING TOOLS AND PROCESSES

Chapter Five

CHAPTER SIX

Acknowledgments

21st Century Selling has been a true collaboration in every good sense of the word. The book would not exist without the contributions and participation of my 14 fellow chapter authors, and I would be remiss in not thanking each of them and expressing my personal and professional respect and admiration.

So thanks (alphabetically) to Scott Bonds, Liz Davidson, Pete Droubay, Dave Greene, Auren Hoffman, Russ and Leslie Knopp, Martyn R. Lewis, Lewis A. Mitchell, Ernest F. Oriente, Dan Seidman, Sandra Swanson, Jeffrey Wildfogel and David Wolf.

Finally, thanks to my editor and colleague, Mark Smith, for his keen eye, creativity and objective advice.

Enjoy the book, and good selling!

Joe Cullinane

Introduction

By Joe Cullinane

Ask any ten sales pros what they think "21st Century Selling" means. Chances are, you'll get ten very different answers.

We asked more than a dozen top sales leaders to share with you their thoughts on "21st Century Selling." We've anthologized their answers and advice in this book. Although they don't agree on everything (and what a surprise it would be if they did), fortunately, you'll find a good deal of consistency in our contributors' perspectives. Much of that consistency is rooted in the importance of understanding and satisfying the buyer.

So what *is* 21st Century Selling? You'll find that it has many facets – understanding the buying cycle, using planning teams, partnering wisely, marketing to niches, using technology-based tools and systems such as e-mail and SFA, understanding the process and costs of acquiring customers, and the overriding importance of creating, building and sustaining relationships with your customers.

Before embarking on this exploration of 21st Century Selling, it's important to recognize what it is not. It is not a substitute for hard work and smart thinking. It is not a panacea or a silver bullet for success. It is not a revolution. But 21st Century Selling is an evolution that combines the best of traditional selling with the new tools available through information technology to create a new model of selling.

In 21st Century Selling, you still need proven sales skills, knowledge and methods. But only when you learn to combine those traditional sales assets with the power of the Internet and other technology-based sales assets will you join the forefront of 21st Century Selling professionals.

We've organized the 14 chapters of our book into three sections: Welcome to the 21st Century, 21st Century Selling Tools and Processes, and Getting It Done in the 21st Century.

Our contributors in Part One include Lewis Mitchell, whose 20-plus-year career in sales and sales management gave him the insights to recognize "It's a Buyer's Market;" Russ and Leslie Knopp, whose consulting practice has shown them the importance of using participative planning teams; Liz Davidson, an entrepreneur who shares her expertise on the subject of partnering; and Pete Droubay, an internationally renowned sales trainer, speaker and author who takes you on a memorable "Sales Odyssey."

In Part Two, you'll share the perspectives of five more contributors, starting with Ernest "The Coach" Oriente, a global expert in sales training and leadership development who offers a variety of practical advice on niche marketing; Dan Seidman, a sales pro, author and consultant who warns of the fine line between writing a proposal and giving a prospect free consulting; Auren Hoffman, an Internet company CEO, entrepreneur and writer who provides wise advice on the advantages of using e-mail; Martyn Lewis, whose examination of "customer acquisition management" helps you understand the process and costs of gaining new customers; and Scott Bonds, an information technology consultant who stresses the importance of building sales-force automation systems to support the needs of the sales force, rather than those of sales management.

Finally, in Part Three, you'll share the experience and insights of contributors Sandra Swanson, a sales executive and an early leader in using the Internet for business and sales, who writes on the subject of customer relationships and satisfaction; Dave Greene, who argues that your job is to help customers understand how they can most effectively get what they want by buying what you're selling; Jeffrey Wildfogel, a Stanford University professor and author who challenges the "time is money" nostrum with the idea that "relationships are money;" and David Wolf, a nationally known sales executive recruiter and consultant who shares the secrets of a sales interview. In a concluding chapter, I offer a summary and provide tips for 21st Century Selling.

Welcome to the world of 21st Century Selling. We hope the ideas and tools presented here will help prepare you for the ride of your life. It's a trip that is just beginning. And its destination is up to you.

PART I

WELCOME TO THE 21ST CENTURY

CHAPTER ONE

It's a Buyer's Market!

Which is to say it's the buyer's buying cycle, not the sales cycle, that controls the transaction. And it's time to start thinking that way.

By Lewis A. Mitchell

Regardless of economic conditions, the complexity of the product or the value of that product, one thing remains constant: it's a buyer's market! Unfortunately, we rarely think that way. But if you change your perspective, you'll have a better opportunity to make more money.

Anyone who has gone through sales training has heard the term "sales cycle." Maybe your employer or co-workers use it. The term, however, is inaccurate. It fails to describe the events that take place before closing a transaction. The prospect's need to proceed through a buying cycle overshadows a salesperson's need to drive a "sales cycle." In the 21st Century, the buyer's buying cycle is what really controls the transaction.

Why is it important to differentiate between a "selling cycle" and a "buying cycle"? Every organization must go through a buying cycle to acquire a product, license a software program or contract for a service offering. Your clients do not have to go through your selling cycle, but they do have to go through their buying cycle. Your prospects aren't interested in what *you* have to do to sell them something. It's not because they don't like you. It's because they have a job to do and don't have the time to reflect on your needs. Your prospects are focused on what *they* have to do.

When I began thinking of my sales efforts from the buyer's point of view, things began to click. I no longer wondered why prospects were acting the way they did. The change in perspective allowed me to anticipate my buyer's next move and to help speed things toward closure. (When using the term "buyer" or "prospect," I am not necessarily referring to an individual but a buying entity made up of a number of individuals who at some point are involved on the buying side of the transaction.) Over the years, I applied this perspective throughout my selling efforts.

When I began managing teams, it was time to document what I had internalized. What helped my teams most to understand the buying process, once they'd changed their perspective, was to track the buyer's internal steps, translating those steps into events that were easily measured, verified or demonstrated. As with anything else, too much of a good thing can lead to disaster. Listing every internal meeting, every internal memo, every funding exercise, etc., would become too cumbersome. Therefore, in developing a list of events, I focused on the milestone events that <u>must</u> occur prior to and just following closing a deal.

The most recent list I developed looked like the one shown below. Although created for software sales, it can be adapted for use with any high-technology product or service. <u>The list is shown in reverse order, beginning at the end of the buying cycle</u>, when all the paperwork has been accounted for, the product shipped and the thank-you letters sent.

BUYING CYCLE EVENTS

- Original Contract is In-House and Product Has Been Shipped (thank-you letters have been sent)
- Date Set for Contract Signing
- Decision Makers Tell Us We've Won/All Approvals Obtained
- All Technical Issues Resolved
- All Business/Contractual Issues Resolved
- Formal Proposal Accepted/Contract Submitted
- All Presentations/Demonstrations/Trials Completed
  HURDLE: Trial Project Plan completed (if a trial is required) and signed by prospect account's project manager as authorized by decision-maker(s).
- Decision Maker(s) Met (conceptual agreement on price and benefit)
  HURDLE: The exact Buying Process is documented (how funded, who signs, who reviews agreements, who approves expenditure, etc.). Are we attached to a

knowledgeable and politically savvy coach? Has that person ever done a deal of this magnitude? What happened the last time this person led this type of project? What stumbling blocks were encountered before completing the agreements for the previous project?

- Project is Funded/Budgeted—Need Established
- Recommender(s) Met/Acquisition Prices Understood/Prospect Committed to an Acquisition Date/Date Validated

The first bullet designates a signed contract submitted to headquarters. The list is set up to remind a sales team to begin with the end in mind—generating revenue for your company. Now let's examine the steps that lead up to a sale.

Before a potential client will buy something from you, that potential client needs to know you exist. For our purposes, I will assume that advertising, seminars, research, direct mail and telemarketing efforts have already occurred and that you have identified a "suspect."

If you have done your homework and qualified a suspect as meeting some fundamental fit criteria, then what you have to offer will save money or increase productivity, revenue or profit (or hit on all four of those items). The suspect doesn't know it yet, but it's only a matter of time before he or she becomes your customer. Using this line of reasoning, the buying cycle begins at that moment in time when a suspect has expressed an interest in your offering and agreed to meet.

Recommender(s) Met/Acquisition Prices Understood/Prospect Committed to an Acquisition Date/Date Validated

During the initial meetings, your job is to evaluate the situation and figure out a time frame. Can the people you're meeting with get the job done? Are your prices within their range? Help them understand that you should be considered a part of their team and that you will act in the interest of their organization. You can't force them to buy if the "fit" isn't right. You don't want to waste their time any more than they will want to waste yours. And if you've been effective in your efforts, you now have a <u>prospect</u> with whom you will proceed through a buying cycle.

It will be in the prospect's best interest to help you decide when the contract will be signed. Ask the following questions: When does this project need to be completed? How long does it take to secure funding? Who reviews the contract, and when should it be submitted? What will happen if the time frame isn't met? Use your experiences as a guide. If the answers you're hearing don't jibe with those experiences, tactfully point out the discrepancies.

Project is Funded/Budgeted — Need Established

Is the project funded/budgeted? Has the need been established and pain been verified? Normally the pain can be established well before the funding mechanism is identified, but these two issues are intertwined. Generally, prospects are willing to pay up front to decrease their pain over time. Define how your product saves them money, makes them more productive or increases their revenues. Help them justify the funding. Ask questions. How is the business case going to be built? Who is responsible for it? When will it be done and approved? Listen to their answers and take the appropriate steps to help them get that business case approved.

No one likes writing a detailed business case, but it is rare that any substantial expenditure is approved without one. If you have a sample that will help your prospect, pass it along. Remember, anything you can do to help your prospect move through the buying cycle faster gives you more padding to hit the established date. I have seen more deals get hung up at the "last minute" due to the lack of a solid business case than for any other reason. Take the time to get it done early and make sure it gets approved.

Now comes the exciting part. It is your job to help your prospect get past the next "event" in the buying cycle. It's your first real hurdle. It's time to document the buying process in writing and in your mind. The best way to do this is to sit with the prospect(s) and look over their organization—understand their business better than they understand it themselves. You are now starting to invest a considerable amount of time into this project, and it's time you nailed everything down. No surprises. Take a moment and reread the questions associated with the first "hurdle" event. Think about and then add any questions that apply to your situation.

Decision Maker(s) Met (conceptual agreement on price and benefit)

Now that you have made it past your first significant hurdle, pat yourself on the back and prepare for your next meeting. You are about to meet with the decision maker and gain tacit approval. It is a great time to make sure the project has the sponsorship it needs before you move to an evaluation or trial period (if such a period is necessary). Make sure you agree on pricing and benefits with the person who will sign the deal. It makes no sense to invest any more effort until that approval is obtained.

The person with the pen has just given the project the go-ahead. Just when you were hoping things were going to get easier, another hurdle looms. This one involves a lot of resources for your company and the prospect. It is a proof-of-concept trial. It's time for you and the prospect to validate that the assumptions made on the technical and business fronts are accurate. In order to do that, you will need to establish success criteria in a formal project plan.

The project plan should outline the technical and business objectives that must be met in order to move forward with the purchase. It must reflect assumptions and account for people, resources, time frames and overall evaluation methodology. It should also include the documented buying process (listing which lawyer will review the agreements and when, which purchasing agent will issue the purchase order and when, who will be responsible for obtaining all necessary approval signatures, who will meet regularly to assess progress, etc.). Most importantly, it needs to be co-authored by you and the prospect. The project plan will need to be signed by representatives of both parties as authorized by the decision maker(s). It should also have provisions for updates and maintenance of the document itself. Finally, someone needs to own this project on the prospect's side. In a perfect world, that person's job should depend on its successful completion. Your job is to make sure you both are successful.

All Presentations/Demonstrations/Trials Completed

Earlier I mentioned that listing every aspect of the buying cycle would lead to disaster. The reason I remind you is that we are covering a lot of effort in one short line: All Presentations/Demonstrations/Trials Completed. It means just what it says — that you have made it to the time to finalize the proposal and make sure that the contract accurately reflects that final proposal.

Formal Proposal Accepted/Contract Submitted

You probably submitted a contract much earlier (at least you should have), and now it's time to make adjustments that reflect the final transaction. Be prepared for the lengthy discussions that may ensue. The prospect will most likely begin posturing for the contractual tug of war as the proposal is reviewed. Make sure you know your limits going in and that you can politely defend all aspects of your final proposal and contract.

All Business/Contractual Issues Resolved

Your goal should be to resolve all the business issues before you tackle any outstanding technical issues. If some technical issues remain unresolved, then expectations must have been incorrectly set at the outset. Your only winning strategy is to believe that the technical issues can be resolved and that wasting time now on those issues isn't productive. It has been my experience that far more deals falter due to irresolvable business and contractual issues (if technical expectations have been set correctly) than due to technical issues. Also, you will most likely have time to fix any technical glitches while the contracts are being shuttled between the two sides.

Decision Maker(s) Tells Us We've Won/All Approvals Obtained

Now things are starting to heat up. You get a call from the decision maker(s) telling you that your team has won and all approvals have been obtained. It's almost time to celebrate. But, being the prudent businessperson you are, you ask when and where the agreements will be signed. You need to have a commitment on a date for that signature. Mark your calendar with an appointment to pick up the agreement or expect a fax moments after the signing, and get your internal paperwork finished and everything prepped for shipment, installation and implementation.

Date Set for Contract Signing

It's that special day and, lo and behold, the deal is signed and it's in your hands. Congratulations, you have nearly completed a buying cycle! Submit the paperwork to Order Entry, Finance, Contracts or whomever is responsible for booking the business in your organization. It's time to sit down and write out the thank-you letters to your teammates. Of course, that team includes your new customer and those people who work for your company that helped make it happen. Now you have completed the Buying Cycle and are well on your way to fantastic success. Good selling!

EPILOGUE

Seeing business transactions from the buyer's perspective will allow you to reach greater heights of success. An ancillary benefit to approaching sales from the buyer's perspective continues on into sales revenue forecasting. It is possible to build a forecasting system that incorporates the Buying Cycle Events list by assigning probabilities to key events. I have built such a system for my teams and found that it yields extremely accurate "no surprises" revenue forecasts. For a copy, visit us at 21stcenturyselling.com.

Lewis "Lewie" Mitchell has been in sales and sales management for nearly 20 years. He started his career with some of the largest high-technology companies in the world, and then began working in high-tech start-ups. He has successfully led both direct and indirect sales organizations, business development, field and corporate marketing, new product introductions, and professional services efforts for those firms.

Seeing unparalleled opportunities in sales after graduating in 1982 with an electrical engineering degree from University of Illinois at Urbana, Mitchell joined the S.T.E.P.S. (Special Training and Experiences in Professional Sales) program being offered by Harris Corporation. S.T.E.P.S. was a year-long immersion designed to take engineers and turn them into businesspeople who could manage Harris' future.

After a successful run at Harris, Mitchell broadened his experience with successes at Dun & Bradstreet and then Xerox Corp. Recruited to Silicon Valley-based Interlink Computer Sciences, Mitchell had his first exposure to the world of startups. He was subsequently recruited to join pre-IPO Mobius Management Systems Inc., which he helped take public in 1998 by leading various sales efforts and by holding such positions as vice president of vertical markets, VP of the Americas and VP of worldwide sales operations. Mitchell is currently executive vice president of sales and marketing for pre-IPO dotLogix, Inc. Over the years Mitchell has received many awards for his sales and management efforts. They include top salesperson honors, manager-of-the-year awards and a forecaster-of-the-year award.

When not leading sales organizations, Mitchell enjoys serving his community, reading, running, barefooting, working out and golfing. He lives just outside Chicago with his wife, their four children and two dogs.

CHAPTER TWO

Participative Planning:
The Competitive Edge

How to build on strengths, identify weaknesses and come up with solutions – in a team format – to achieve outstanding results.

By Russ and Leslie Knopp

In the 21st Century competitive arena, where customer choice is a given, effective sales planning that provides the ultimate flexibility to meet customer needs is essential. Now is the time for a proven, successful model known as participative planning to yield its impressive results in the sales arena. From small family businesses to Fortune 500 companies, businesses that have used participative planning techniques, initially developed more than 35 years ago, have achieved outstanding results.

In her book *Winning Through Participation*, Laura J. Spencer reported many interesting examples of such results. The McDonald's Corp., for one, increased sales 10 percent to 20 percent in markets where managers and franchise owners applied these methods. Also a subsidiary of Sun Chemical Company of New York increased its sales by 40 percent in just six months. And one of Japan's Nichii Department Stores raised its sales rating from 37th to 15th within a year of instituting participative planning techniques.

Participative planning gets employees involved in planning and problem-solving tasks. This kind of involvement animates and inspires both individuals and groups. With participative planning, employees actively work together to develop plans, and they become highly motivated to carry them out successfully. This surge of energy and commitment results in improved performance and ongoing enthusiasm, both of which are essential for success in today's environment. Leaders and managers can put participative planning into action by following these guidelines.

THE PARTICIPATIVE-PLANNING PROCESS

Successful sales planning is done by a team representing all the people, units or functions that will have an impact on achieving sales or that will be affected by the successful sales program. Assemble a planning team that consists not only of members of the sales team itself, but also of people who represent functions that will help or hinder the sales team's efforts. To identify potential team members, think about:

- What departments does the sales team depend on to deliver on promises made or for information?
- If the sales program brings in new business, what functions or departments will be affected?

A planning team with appropriate representation will develop a realistic, achievable plan that builds on strengths and addresses inherent and potential challenges. The team will create better plans and solutions because the process allows members to share ideas, think creatively and build new synergies.

Participative sales planning involves five major steps:
1. establish the context for planning
2. create a practical vision of success for a specified time period
3. examine the underlying contradictions to the vision of success
4. develop an integrated strategy
5. develop a tactical plan to implement the strategy and achieve the vision

These steps result in a plan that is comprehensive and far reaching, while at the same time so specific that implementation may begin immediately when the plan is complete. It provides a framework that allows flexibility and encourages responsiveness to new opportunities and challenges. Once the planning team is in place and preparation done, and with the assistance of a skilled facilitator, the following steps may be completed in a retreat setting or in a series of shorter planning sessions.

ESTABLISH THE CONTEXT FOR PLANNING

All team members should understand the context in which planning is taking place. The context includes current and past sales data and other facts along with existing perceptions, future opportunities and trends. In this step, these elements are brought to light and assessed in relation to the company, product, service or industry. Begin by examining what is working well internally. What recent successes has the company experienced? Who are the new customers? How were these relationships developed? Where have new solutions for customers been devised, large margins achieved, sales projections exceeded? Identify what has worked well to inform thinking about how to build on current strengths.

Examining the challenges to a successful sales program is equally important. What are the internal factors that are inhibiting growth, profit or sales? Are there internal systems issues to address? Is the product or service meeting customers' current needs? Is the pricing competitive and appropriate? Are the marketing strategy and advertising messages effective? What are the internal givens that are unchangeable? Policy? Price? Product? After examining challenges, the planning team can then either identify solutions to the challenges or ways to get around them.

Customer perceptions can be your greatest ally or enemy in the sales process. Do you know what perceptions your customers have about your product, your service, the people they have contact with in your company, your company or even the industry itself? Many organizations complete periodic customer satisfaction surveys, focus groups and other forms of feedback. The sales team should review this information and develop a thorough understanding of customer perceptions as well as their anticipated needs. This will allow the team to develop sales strategies that build on positive positions and address perceived weaknesses.

External forces will also have an impact on your sales success. Differentiate yourself by understanding the competition and using these insights to develop the sales plan. Ask, "Who are our competitors?" "What are their strengths and weaknesses?" Social, industry and market trends also will have a major impact on your success and should be considered in developing the sales plan. Other questions members of the planning team should research and discuss in preparation for planning include:

- Where is your industry heading?
- What consumer or business trends will impact the sales process, the customers, the end-users?
- What impact have recent technological advancements had on the sales process and on your customers?
- Are lifestyle changes a consideration?
- Are there regulatory issues to account for?

Use any and all forms of market intelligence available, such as sales-records analysis, market research and customer feedback in preparation for planning. The process of developing and presenting the information that establishes the context for planning may be assigned to individual team members. Many organizations assign these tasks to internal departments or hire consultants for expertise and advice. The important thing is to establish a context for planning that is grounded in a thorough understanding of the current situation and informed predictions about the short-term future.

CREATE A PRACTICAL VISION OF SUCCESS

The team must now articulate a shared, practical vision of success within a specific time period. This vision answers the question, "What does success look like three or five years from now?" Is it customers who depend on you for solutions and recognize the value of the salesperson? Does it include moving current customers to a higher level of relationship and purchasing? Do you envision meeting or exceeding sales quotas and goals? By identifying each team member's specific images of success, the group can form a common, practical vision of the future. This vision provides the direction for alignment of internal strategies. When a vision is clearly articulated, a focused strategy can then be developed. When a regional Big Brothers Big Sisters organization articulated its vision to double the number of children served in three years, it was able to align fundraising, volunteer recruitment and case management strategies to achieve the vision.

Clearly articulated visions are extremely powerful and motivating. They emerge from deeply held hopes, dreams and aspirations of individuals. When stated objectively, visions provide fuel, energy and endurance for people, teams and organizations. Individual and shared visions grow as people do. Therefore, the visioning process is a dynamic one, and the vision should be rearticulated as appropriate. For most companies and organizations, the vision is reviewed annually and revised or completely redone upon completion of the strategic plan.

EXAMINE THE UNDERLYING CONTRADICTIONS

Once you have articulated the common, practical vision of what the successful future looks like, you can identify the contradictions or barriers to achieving the vision. The question answered by this process is: "What obstacles or roadblocks may keep us from realizing our vision of success?" These barriers are like boulders in the pathway. They are so integrated with our daily experience that we do not always recognize them as barriers.

Contradictions are found in historic and societal trends, images and attitudes, and in structures and patterns. Barriers to successful sales can be found in situations such as internal systems that don't lend themselves to meeting customers' changing needs, outmoded processes that slow delivery, or perceptions about limitations of the sales force, product or service. When looking for contradictions, examine recent failures and identify patterns of success or failure. A regional utility provider found that a complicated billing system was confusing customers who purchased both gas and electric services. Consequently, customers were opting out. Pinpointing this concern allowed the company to address and resolve the problem with upgraded computer technology and software. Ask: "Why did we lose that order? Why did we miss that opportunity? What happened to cause us to lose that customer?" Look beyond the obvious to the underlying reasons for problems.

After examining individual situations and incidents, the team will be able to identify patterns and draw conclusions about barriers to achieving the vision. These contradictions are not always obvious in the beginning. But if they are not identified, they can defeat the team. Honest, thoughtful consideration of the contradictions allows the organization to improve continuously.

DEVELOP THE STRATEGY

Setting strategic direction is a pivotal point in the planning process. This is the beginning of creating an action plan. So far the planning team will have used both visionary and analytical thinking. Now it is time to call upon the team's skills in strategic and creative thinking. Strategies are broad directions for action that will help to overcome a contradiction and will catalyze movement toward the vision. Strategies for action may address and remove a contradiction head-on, such as the example of the utility provider with the faulty billing system. Other strategies may be indirect, circumventing an unchangeable contradiction. For example, when the same utility provider found that state regulations prohibited sharing customer information across subsidiaries, they implemented a new community-relations program to create awareness of their offerings. Strategies often take the form of a new program, project, course of action or system. They tend to be broad and comprehensive, and they are as likely to focus inward as outward. They are effective because they are strategic, rather than individual actions and lists of "things to do."

Creativity and innovation are key to developing an effective strategy. Solutions that address, either directly or indirectly, more than one of the contradictions, or barriers, are the most catalytic. With just a few well-conceived strategies, a sales team, company or organization can overcome multiple problems and move swiftly toward achieving its goals. A multistate retail organization successfully instituted for its supervisors a training program on employee evaluation. The program addressed multiple barriers including internal employee-relations issues and external issues related to employee interactions with customers.

The strategy acts like a rudder, orienting the company and team to a particular direction and focusing change. People who participate in the creation of strategies experience a sense of ownership and feel that they can make a valuable contribution to its successful implementation. At this point, planning team participants begin thinking about specific things they can do to accomplish the strategies. These thoughts are the beginnings of the implementation plan.

DEVELOP THE IMPLEMENTATION PLAN

The implementation plan is a set of specific tactics and actions designed to initiate movement from where the group is today to where it hopes to be in the future. It provides a clear description of what the action steps are, why they are necessary, who will do them, how they will be done, and when and where they will be accomplished. In many traditional sales planning processes, this is the step when the manager, team or salesperson begins to plan. With the participative planning method, the actions to be implemented are directed toward a common vision of success and are structured to address barriers to the vision, rather than in isolation from these factors that are so critical to overall success.

The implementation plan has two parts. It establishes the major actions and quarterly benchmarks for the coming 12 months, and it details the first-quarter plan that will launch implementation of the strategy. At this time the planning team sets goals. These include traditional sales measurements such as new customers, greater penetration per account, volume increases or market share. This is the time to set annual, quarterly and monthly sales goals.

Major actions to address barriers and implement the strategy also are determined at this time. These actions are specific and concrete. For example, if a team has identified a barrier such as an inadequate understanding of customer needs, it may decide to initiate monthly customer focus groups as a specific tactic. The actions in the implementation plan have an end point, can be accomplished within a specific time period, and are measurable.

Once the major goals and actions are in place, it is time to select first-quarter actions and to clarify the who, how, what, why and where they will be done. The first step in this process is to determine the priority of the major actions. Typically, there are certain actions that should be implemented before others because they will impact other parts of the plan. When prioritizing actions, the team asks: "Which are the most urgent? Which will be easiest to accomplish and therefore will generate momentum? Which will pave the way for other successes?" Once the team selects first-quarter actions, it sequences tactical steps, determines resource needs, and selects measurements.

The implementation plan creates action. When implementation is underway, it creates reaction and response. It brings the strategies into reality and exposes them as either effective or defective. In this way, the implementation plan is a learning process and an evaluation tool. It generates new data and creates new questions, which can then be used to inform ongoing decisions and planning.

WINNING THROUGH PARTICIPATIVE PLANNING

Participative sales planning follows a process that begins with developing a common vision of success and ends with the construction of an implementation plan complete with benchmarks, assignments and deadlines. Although the process is most often facilitated by outside consultants, members of the planning team make the decisions. Decisions are based upon current realities of the business and are practical and doable.

Companies that employ participative sales planning experience five major benefits:

1. The specific plans, strategies, solutions and action plans are flexible, appropriate and achievable, often resulting in improvement throughout the entire organization.

2. Employees who participate in the process develop greater commitment and ability to implement decisions and strategies. Individuals often discover untapped talents and develop new skills during planning and implementation.

3. The process generates a greater portfolio of innovative ideas, often resulting in new solutions to long-standing concerns.

4. A common framework develops for decision making, communication, planning and problem solving. Cross-functional efficiency, an effective monitoring system and faster turnaround times are just a few of the ways this framework benefits a company.

5. The shared understanding of the vision of success and strategy to get there encourages individual initiative and responsibility and develops the kind of teamwork in which the whole is truly greater than the sum of the parts.

It's important to remember that a good participative-planning process is not enough by itself. The successful implementation of participative planning connects directly to several organizational factors. To foster successful participation, and to make the most of plans developed, leaders and sales managers must continually focus on four key success factors:

- Fostering open communication through formal and informal processes
- Encouraging people to set and reach high performance goals
- Empowering people with the resources, knowledge and support that allows initiative and creativity in problem solving
- Rewarding and recognizing strategic contributions

Russ and Leslie Knopp have consulted with hundreds of businesses, schools and nonprofit organizations individually and together for more than 10 years. They own Traverse Management Resources Inc., an organization that was created to help people and their organizations envision their desired destination, plot the course and navigate changing conditions to get there.

Trained in the facilitation methods developed by the Institute of Cultural Affairs, the Knopps are members of the International Association of Facilitators. Russ' professional roots are anchored in a successful sales career, in which he identified clients' needs and provided creative solutions. His corporate management experiences include training, marketing, staff development, and developing business plans and strategies to increase profitability and market penetration. Before founding Traverse Management Resources Inc., Leslie owned and operated Initiatives, a consulting firm specializing in educational partnerships, with a focus on collaborative strategic planning. Her background is in education, as a teacher of secondary and adult students, partnership director and administrator with responsibility for internal and external communications.

Contact:

Russ and Leslie Knopp

Traverse Management Resources Inc.

1211 E. Front St., Suite 233

Traverse City, MI 49686

Phone: 231-947-9477

E-mail: lknopp@traverse.com

Web site: www.tmrfacilitators.com

CHAPTER THREE

To Partner or Not to Partner?

That is the question. The answer is absolutely. But smart partnering demands you do it at the right time with realistic expectations.

By Liz Davidson

T oday partnerships are more crucial than ever, to the point that they can determine the success or failure of a company. And yet most companies lose money through their partnerships.

At my company, Financial Finesse, we've learned from our partnerships — learned our limits as a firm and how we can work with larger companies to sell, market and, in some cases, develop our products and services. As a financial education company, we provide unbiased financial education content to groups, associations and consumers. We deliver our content through live seminars, online financial platforms that our client companies plug into their intranets, online seminars, a help line for corporations and consumers, a radio show and our Web site. We've learned how to reach and influence potential customers about our services without spending millions of dollars on sales and marketing. Some partners have burned us. We've hit the jackpot with others. Most importantly, we've learned how to partner for growth.

As an entrepreneur with an MBA, an investment banking background and a blatant disregard for both, I've learned how crucial it is to employ people who know things I don't. As a result, I believe it's important that my company partner with other firms to compensate for our own weakness as an organization. In the course of building two companies, I've learned there is a limit to what one person or even what one company can achieve.

Hopefully you can heed our hard-earned wisdom to avoid costly mistakes and achieve huge wins for your company. To be far ahead of most companies, all you have to do is follow three simple rules.

TIP 1: KNOW WHY, WHO AND WHEN

In the massive optimism of the dot-com era, firms partnered constantly without knowing or caring why. The thought was that if you could issue a press release stating that you had partnered with Yahoo, AOL, Amazon or even smaller portals or dot-com companies with name recognition, you would increase the chances of emerging in your category.

Now that the bubble has burst and partnerships have fallen apart, often due to one or both companies going out of business or "changing their strategy" (a euphemism for finding a business model so they can pay their employees), "casual" partnering is outdated. And companies increasingly realize how expensive it is. Relationship management takes time, often on the part of a team of employees, and carries an inherent opportunity cost. If your people are wasting time on partnerships that don't generate revenue, don't help you produce a better product, or only marginally raise your brand awareness or loyalty, you are losing money. You are facing two costs in this scenario. First, you are not making the money you would through the right partnerships. Second, you are losing the money you are paying employees who are establishing and managing the wrong partnerships.

How can you effectively partner with companies to grow your business significantly? The key lies in upfront research and planning to ensure your partnerships are with the right people, under the right terms and conditions, at the right time in your company's life and with the right objective.

The first step is to define why you want to partner at all. What does your company need that it can't provide for itself? With most firms in this economy, the answer is distribution. An internal sales force can be highly effective, but there is no real leverage. One person can sell only so much. A distributor who touches thousands, tens of thousands, possibly millions of customers, can extend your reach beyond your greatest expectations.

In our experience at Financial Finesse, you can't have too many distribution relationships, particularly if your distributors are paying you to resell your product or service or, better yet, buying inventory and then reselling it.

Other compelling reasons to partner are marketing support, product development support, product fulfillment and bundling. At times, these reasons are more compelling than distribution relationships, particularly for larger companies. There is no rule as to the best reason to partner—the only rule here is that you need to have a good reason.

The next step is to determine who best can fulfill your partnership needs. Don't limit yourself. Although it's difficult to manage too many partnerships, those that generate significant revenue are almost always worth the time spent managing them. To start thinking about potential targets, ask yourself a few questions: Which companies have considerable strengths in your area of weakness? What is their track record for developing partnerships? Do your due diligence here. Some companies have a track record for "eating" their competitors — that is, stealing their business concepts and putting them out of business. Other companies — Cisco Systems and AOL come to mind — are much more partnership minded and can help your company grow.

The last part of the equation is when to begin the process of soliciting a potential partner. Small companies have a particularly hard time with this as they often get overzealous to approach big-name partners, hoping that establishing a partnership will put them on the map, help them attract additional funding and possibly enable them to achieve profitability. They will contact every major company in an industry, desperate for partners, but without a clear understanding of what their own firm can bring to the partnership. The big companies almost invariably turn down the opportunity to partner. Even worse, they often form negative opinions that preclude them from establishing a partnership at a later date when the startup is more ready.

On the other hand, you have to be careful not to wait too long, particularly in light of long lead times with larger firms. (More on this in Tip No. 2.)

When is the right time? The answer isn't as clear as we'd like. In fact, it's more a question of approach than timing. If you want to get a large distribution deal with a major player in your industry, begin by networking with different distributors at industry conferences and events. Let them know what your company does and what you are looking for in a partner. Then watch their reaction. Are they excited by your idea? Do they offer their business cards and suggest setting up a meeting, or are they lukewarm? Use their reactions as a guide to tell you whether or not you are ready.

Friends and "friendlies" are also excellent resources. If you're unsure your company is ready to approach a major player, search your contacts to see if you can set up a meeting with an acquaintance who works at the firm you are interested in partnering with or who has contacts in the industry. Use these contacts to establish an initial meeting. Friends and acquaintances are much more likely to give you an honest answer as to how seriously their firms would consider your proposal, and they can provide feedback on how to improve your pitch. Better yet, they will not hold your own ignorance against you later and can become valuable advocates for your firm within their organizations.

TIP 2: HAVE A VISION — AND CONFIDENCE

Don't grossly exaggerate your company's projections or evade questions about your company's current situation. Instead, rely on statistics, such as your current growth rate, customer retention, Web site traffic, etc., to support your case. Determine what your company is doing right, and use this to show your partners that your company will be a powerhouse.

We've always done this well at Financial Finesse. As a result, we've established partnerships with companies more than 100 times our size — companies that have significant resources to promote our products and services and are willing to risk their time, effort and money on doing so based on our potential as an organization. We reached an agreement with a leading online financial-calculator firm to pay us to resell our content and, better yet, to bundle it with their tools. Another important early partner, an online human resources firm with access to more than two million small-business owners, traded significant cash and marketing support in exchange for sponsorship of Financial Finesse's programs, events and media. Companies such as Macy's and Reebok, as well, have partnered with Financial Finesse in our early days because they saw the company as offering a unique benefit to their users.

In each case, we first had to figure out what our potential partners were looking for from us and then determine how we could best meet their needs. Sometimes the reason was emotional—they believed fervently in financial education and wanted to align their companies with this value. Other times, they were interested in our high user demographics and loyalty. Increasingly, the reason has been our award-winning financial education content. Content is scarce these days with dot-coms folding. Quality content is even scarcer.

In all these situations, we've had to show where we are today and where we plan to be in the future. We've used historical growth rates to project future growth, and new product demos to show how our content will evolve in the future, as well as customer case studies and endorsements to show how we've built and continue to build brand recognition and loyalty. Sometimes we've even shared elements of our business plan.

And we've always made our case with passion, conviction and confidence that belied our size. We knew who we were, where we were going, how we were different and why we were important. That's why the firms we wanted to partner with chose to work with us over competitors with greater resources and name recognition.

TIP 3: HOLD PARTNERS TO HIGH STANDARDS

When we started partnering with firms at Financial Finesse, we made the mistake of treating our partners like customers. We focused nearly all our energy on what we could do for them, rather than making sure they met their commitments and obligations to us. The result was that we had excellent relationships with partners who loved working with us but consistently took advantage of us. Those who promised to distribute did so sporadically, choosing to focus instead on partners who were twisting their arms. The same thing happened with those who promised to market our services. The efforts were careless at best, visibility was below our expectations, and we often ended up unofficially dissolving the partnership in search of partners we could hold accountable from the start.

We learned from our mistakes, and you can, too. Today, we have three steadfast rules for partnering to ensure that our partners are meeting their end of the bargain:

> 1. Set revenue goals with all distribution partnerships, deadlines and deliverables with all product development partnerships, and lead generation goals with all marketing relationships.
>
> 2. Set quarterly or monthly meetings to review progress against these goals. As the CEO, I generally attend these meetings.
>
> 3. Establish the right to terminate the contract within 30 days if the goals are not met. This way, time and money won't be spent on relationships that aren't worth it.

Sounds simple, but the vast majority of companies, particularly young companies, neglect these steps. By not setting expectations, they ensure having none. When they let their partners off the hook, the partnership is taken less seriously.

To partner or not to partner? Today, in order to develop a high-end product offering with limited time, money and resources, you have to partner. You simply can't do it all internally. The question becomes, "How to partner?"

Partnering is about knowing what you need, where to get it, what you can give in return, and how to set and manage expectations so that your partners keep their commitments. It is a three-step process that entails research, selling and management. Each step is crucial, but none is sufficient on its own. Most companies only do one or two and end up wasting huge amounts of money on a lot of fruitless business relationships. They sign many contracts but make little progress. If you can master the three steps outlined in this chapter, your firm will have an edge that could propel it to the top of its industry. You'll be able to do more with less, and in today's economy, the ability to achieve greatness with limited resources will separate the winners from the losers.

Liz Davidson is the founder and CEO of Financial Finesse. Before founding Financial Finesse, Liz successfully founded and managed Davidson Andrade, an investment company with more than $35 million under management.

Liz has a strong passion for helping people everywhere gain financial independence and security, and she has achieved national prominence as a speaker, radio show host and frequently quoted expert on investment matters.

In 2001, Liz was awarded Working Woman's regional "Entrepreneurial Excellence" Award for an Innovative Product or Service. A nationally recognized expert on investing and financial planning, she has been profiled and/or interviewed by *Forbes*, NBC Nightly News, CNBC, ZDTV, *The Wall Street Journal Online*, *BusinessWeek*, *Working Woman*, *Cosmopolitan*, *Inc.*, the *Chicago Tribune*, the *LA Times*, *Access Magazine*, *Employee Benefits News*, *Investment News*, the *Boston Globe*, *Entrepreneur's Business Start Ups*, *Entrepreneur Illustrated*, *TechWeek*, *Sales and Marketing Management*, *Financial Services Marketing*, and the KTLA Morning News, among others. As a former hedge fund manager, she is quoted extensively in *The Unofficial Guide to Investing in Mutual Funds* and was instrumental in providing proprietary investment research to the book's author.

Prior to founding Davidson Andrade and Financial Finesse, Liz was an investment banker in Smith Barney's corporate finance department, working on initial public offerings, mergers and acquisitions, private equity deals, and debt issuances.

Liz holds an MBA in finance from the Anderson School UCLA and a B.A. in American studies with a concentration in economics from Davidson College.

CHAPTER FOUR

A 21st Century Selling Odyssey

In the new century, it's not about one sale anymore.
It's about acquiring a client for many journeys together.

By Pete Droubay

"Care to see the future?" the voice asked.

The question startled me. My jaunt into cyberspace had been a diversion, an escape. The dizzying lights and carnival atmosphere were just what I needed to take my mind off a tough sales month. Meeting quotas and, even harder, getting people to buy from me felt overwhelming. I had been to so many sales seminars — Jay Douglas Edwards, Tom Hopkins, Dale Carnegie — and I felt like a phony. So I had found myself some distraction, as I was doing most nights that month. A little distraction is good for you, I reasoned. It relaxes you. Lets you forget how badly things are going.

But now I was alert again, startled by a question from a man who had appeared to me amid the noise and the lights.

"Care to see the future?" He raised one eyebrow and put his hands in the pockets of some very well-tailored slacks.

I couldn't help smirking. "The future? You want to tell my fortune?"

"No," he said, "I won't tell you about the future; I'll have you experience it firsthand."

"What, you want to send me into the future? Sell me a time machine?"

The guy only smiled again.

"Not a time machine, but a doorway of sorts. Where I come from, we don't sell machines; we sell experiences. So let me ask you, how would it change your life to glimpse the 21st Century?"

I thought about my current stressful circumstances, the pressure I was under to get people to say "yes," the monthly uncertainty of how much I was going to produce, and I thought that at worst this would be an interesting distraction. At best, it would give me some certainty.

"How much?" I asked.

"Just a few dollars."

"You're kidding. There's no way that's profitable for you. You're trying to scam me."

"Nope. Where I come from, the cost of production is very low, so I can charge a lot less than you think. I'll let you pay me when your glimpse is over. If you liked the experience, I'll collect a fee; if not, then it's free."

"You're offering me credit and a guarantee, and you don't even know my name! You've got to be one of the worst businessmen I've ever met!"

He didn't look the least insulted. "Oh, I know who you are. I wouldn't have approached you unless I knew all about you and knew you could benefit from my services, as well as pay for them. You see, where I come from, information about you and all of my other clients is readily available. So what will it be? A glimpse into the future, or stay struggling here in your past?"

I was intrigued by this man. He wasn't the greatest businessman and not even a great salesperson (as if the two were different). But he was captivating. Maybe I'd take a chance.

"Okay," I said, "I'll take you up on the offer. Where can you send me?"

"I'll start by taking you to my time. The 21st Century." He gestured toward a doorway, and I followed him as he stepped through it. As I passed the threshold, I felt odd, dizzy.

Then I was standing in a room that looked like an office lobby. It looked no different from any room I might have occupied in my own time while waiting to see a client. On the wall a sign read, "21st Century Sales Company."

A woman's voice came from all around me. "Mr. Jenkins, you're next. You may step in now for your interview."

What interview? I thought as I stepped through the doorway in front of me. Suddenly I stood in a traditional executive office, no different from what I was used to seeing in the 20th Century. A handsome, fit man in his 50s stepped around the desk to shake my hand.

"So you're Jenkins! Jim tells me you may become one of our best salespeople yet. He's told me such good things about you that I'm excited about this interview! It always helps to have his recommendation when applying for a job here. If only the other 2,000 applicants I reviewed today understood the power of association, they might have gotten through the door. But they're stuck in the last century. I mean, how do they expect to compete in the 21st Century Sales Company if they can't even make friends with one of our top people and get their recommendation before applying?"

My mind was spinning, trying to place everything he said into some kind of context. I was applying for a sales position? Just my luck, I thought. I step into the future to apply for a job I already hate.

But then I got to wondering. How had he reviewed 2,000 applications today? That was impossible. And why were there no other applicants in the lobby?

"Am I the only one you're interviewing?" I asked.

He laughed and slapped me on the back. "I like a sense of confidence! Of course not. I've got interviews all day. Everyone wants to work for the 21st Century Sales Company. Most everyone these days realizes that we're all salespeople in life, anyway."

A 21st Century Selling Odyssey

"Everyone's a salesperson?" I asked, thinking this guy was crazier than the last one.

He laughed again. "Young man, I can see why Jim likes you. You're quick to call me on my exaggerations. You're right. We're not quite there yet, but we will be soon. There are still people out there who don't get it, but they won't be around much longer. I just talked to my parents' doctor the other day, and he was complaining about business being down because of so much competition. I started to give him some marketing tips, but he cut me off, saying he wasn't a salesperson and didn't want to talk about my far-fetched ideas. Unfortunately, he'll either have to retire or learn to compete by selling and marketing his services. Of course, he'd have to brush up on all the new technology that would practice medicine for him. After all, the real work these days is done by technology, and we humans are left to persuade people to use it. But he hasn't spent the time to learn about the technology, so even if he tried to market himself, he'd struggle because he doesn't have that competitive advantage."

So competition and technology have turned everyone into salespeople, I thought. But the man before me still hadn't answered my question. Why hadn't I seen anyone else? No one had even come out of his office before me.

"So where's everyone else?" I asked.

"Everyone who?"

"All the other applicants."

"Oh, they're all over the globe. I don't even ask where they're from."

"But why weren't they in the lobby?"

He laughed again. "Jim was right. You're brilliant! I like your sense of humor. Who did you want to see in your lobby? You're the one who set it up, and I have no idea what it looks like." He paced, stroking his chin with one hand. "What a brilliant screening tool! To see each applicant's layout for the lobby and the office might give me a sense of his or her psychology. I hadn't thought about it before. Until now, I've just assumed each person was sitting at home in their underwear, and I left it at that. I never thought about how someone constructed the lobby, the office, and even me, for that matter!"

Now I was really confused.

"So why should I hire you?" he asked, his face now cool and analytical, one eyebrow rising up again.

My mind was blank. Then I blurted out, "Because I work hard."

He guffawed and slapped his knee. "Son, you're a born comedian. I haven't heard that one in a long time! Everyone knows that no one cares about your hard work. All we want to know is what results you'll produce. But tell you what. Time grows short, so maybe it's best for me to tell you about the proposal you'll need to put together and present to me at the next interview to get a job with the 21st Century Sales Company."

Wow, I thought. Getting a job here is like selling a large contract to a client. It's like I own my own company. This is serious stuff.

"So listen up and take notes if you need to," he said. "We've divided the sales process into six areas of focus. Your proposal to me will need to highlight what you have to offer us in each of these areas. In fact, I have a little acronym to help you remember the six areas. The acronym sounds like "Megasales," but it's spelled M-G-S-A-L-S. Each one of the letters stands for a step in the sales process and a set of skills you must show us you've mastered."

For the first time I noticed big brass letters on the wall of his office spelling out MGSALS.

MODEL THE BEST

"The M stands for Model the Best. We'll begin by taking a look at how you model the character of the best salespeople in the world. This includes, first, your commitments and your personal standards. We want to know that they are much higher than the average person's. Second, your ability to manage your mental and emotional states in a positive way. Third, your reasons or motivations for doing well. Fourth, your beliefs about what you do and how you do it. And fifth, how organized you are and how well you manage your time and your resources."

If I get this job, I thought, the days of getting drunk at the office party because I'm depressed, the days of feeling uninspired and being behind on everything and hating what I do, were over. These people want me to be a better person! I pulled out a notepad I didn't know I had and began writing. I didn't even think of sitting down.

GENERATE LEADS

"The G stands for Generate Leads," he went on. "I want to know that you can put yourself in a position where you have more people to talk to than you could ever possibly contact, more qualified leads than you could ever help out. That's a great position to be in, and I want you to show me how you'll create that. This includes, first, your ability to identify an ideal client and build a database of qualified leads and, second, your ability to establish yourself to those ideal clients as an expert. Third, I want to see multiple lead-generation systems to reach your ideal clients and, fourth, I want to see that you understand the power of systems and know how to systematize each lead-generation method. Fifth, show us how you plan on measuring your success and managing it."

So much for showing up to work and waiting for a client to magically appear, I thought as I furiously scribbled on the notepad.

SET APPOINTMENTS

He leaned back against his desk. "The first S stands for Set Appointments. You must be able to engage each one of your leads and set up an appointment to offer your services. I want you first to show us how you plan to build quick rapport with each client. Second, show us how you'll create each client's interest for your products. Third, demonstrate effectiveness on the telephone. Fourth, show us how you'll manage your schedule and your territory. Finally, fifth, show us how you'll leverage your time by having your schedule filled up for you."

Uh-oh. I guess "winging it" is no longer an acceptable practice. I was starting to get writer's cramp, but I kept writing.

ACCESS LEVERAGE

He went on. "The A stands for Access Leverage. You must be able to under-stand what's going to move each client. In other words, what's the leverage for each client? I want to see that you, first, know how to create long-term rela-tionships with your clients; second, that you understand why people buy and that you can ask appropriate questions; third, how you will do a great needs analysis with each client; fourth, how you can find a client's rules, values and global beliefs; and fifth, that you determine a client's habitual ways of think-ing — also called metaprograms — and can sell based on them."

I was squirming now. But I kept writing.

LAY OUT YOUR OFFER

He strolled to the window, then turned to face me. "The L stands for Lay Out Your Offer. You must be able to lay out a great offer. One that's com-pelling and exciting to each individual client you work with. We'll obviously judge your ability to do this based on how you deliver your presentation to us. We want to see that, first, you can set the stage for a great presentation — in other words that you can preheat or preframe the situation. Second, we want to see that you can focus on benefits rather than just facts and, third, that you understand and can use test closes. Fourth, we want to see you struc-ture, from beginning to end, a dynamic presentation and, fifth, see that you can speak in front of people."

SEAL THE DEAL

He came back to where I stood scribbling. "And then finally, you must also be able to Seal the Deal, which is the final S. And that means first, handling objections; second, closing the sale in such a way that it's easy, painless and exciting to buy what you're offering; third, eliminating any buyer's remorse; fourth, conducting great client follow-up and; fifth, getting the next sale."

He looked me in the eye. "Make sure you present your talents and skills in this order, because context is so important. Don't be like those fools in the last century who were proud of the fact that they could close a sale, but hadn't given any thought to generating leads or any other aspect of the sales process. Your presentation doesn't have to be long, just specific. I hate generalities and clichés."

"I was hoping for a little on-the-job training," I said.

He laughed so hard he couldn't talk for a minute. "There's that sense of humor again! No one does that anymore, especially when we're paying millions of dollars a year to people who hardly lift a finger. No, they'd better be prepared before they walk in here. Well, Jenkins, we're out of time, but get your presentation ready, and I'll see you at our next meeting."

MANY JOURNEYS TOGETHER

A million dollars per year for hardly lifting a finger? But before I could ask more about the compensation, I found myself standing outside the original door with Jim, surrounded by all the colorful, dizzying lights again.

"So," he asked, "are you ready to go to work on your proposal?"

"I'm not sure I can give the presentation he wants."

"That's where I can help," he said. "In our next journey together, I'll help you put together the first part of the proposal."

"Next journey?"

"In the 21st Century our relationship doesn't end here. You are now my client, and we'll have the pleasure of many journeys together."

"How can you be so certain?"

"Don't worry. In the 21st Century the responsibility for the contact has shifted from the consumer to the salesperson. I can't afford to wait and hope that you make it back to me. I'd go broke."

"That's ridiculous! You've got my money, and as soon as you're out of sight, I'll never see you again."

"You believe that because you still think the first sale should be your focus. "

"But I know you were focused on selling to me."

"Of course I was, but not because of the profit I'm hoping to earn from this first experience. I haven't even begun to recoup my acquisition costs."

"Your what?"

"The amount of money I spend to acquire each client."

"Do you mean you spent more than those few dollars to get me into your time machine?"

"Well, not you specifically, but if you divide my total advertising and sales budget by my number of clients and add to that my time, which I value a lot higher than your generation ever did, I'm currently at a loss."

"Then why do it?"

"Because it's not about one sale anymore. It's about acquiring a client. Once I acquire a client I know that the lifetime value of my average client is huge, because of all of the other products and services that they and other clients will buy. For instance, I know that you'll enjoy glimpses into the future many more times. I know that you'll bring friends with you each time you come, and I also know how many. I know that as you glimpse the future, you'll ask me to serve you in one of the many other ways that I can, and we'll enjoy years of service agreements and contracts."

"I think I understand, but still, wouldn't it be better to charge more on the first visit and make money on it, too? After all, it was certainly worth it. I would have paid more, and I'm sure you've got the sales skills to twist my arm to do it."

"I could get *you* to pay more," he said. "But if I did, would you feel compelled to come back? Besides, in the 21st Century my competitors and I all have access to cheap money and inexpensive financing, and we're able to offer prices as low as what I've offered you. Some even offer it for lower."

"Yeah, but I don't know any of your competitors. You could have easily charged me more, and I wouldn't have known the difference."

"That's because you still live in the 20th Century. In my time there are only few people like that left. Those who try to make a living by overcharging clients lead wretched lives themselves, waiting for easy prey, swooping in for the kill and then hoping never to see those clients again. Most of them are broke, living month to month, hoping that next month will be the big score, but knowing inside that it won't be. They're a dying breed. They move from one job to another in companies and industries that haven't figured out how to enter the 21st Century."

I had the eerie feeling that he was describing me. The memories came flooding back to me of months in my sales career when the fear of not earning money drove me to "make a deal at any cost." Along with them came the pangs of guilt that I had always felt when I made deals that were in my best interest but not the client's.

Jim continued. "No, the relationship is what I'm after. I know that you'll pay me for many years to come. And my costs for maintaining our relationship will be minimal."

"It's gotta cost you something to get me back here. I mean, I'm not even sure where I am, and if you expect me to come back, you're going to have to put up some major signs with directions."

"There you go again, thinking like the 20th Century. You won't need to find me; I'll find you. You won't need to call me, and you'll never need to visit my office. But I'll constantly be setting and keeping appointments with you."

I looked around me. "Uh, how do I get home from here?"

He laughed. "Home! You are home! In fact, you never left. But then that's an illusion that you'll understand only when you step into the 21st Century."

Peter Droubay is a speaker and corporate trainer who has given more than 3,000 workshops, classes and speeches to clients such as Mazda, OfficeMax,

Watkins, IBM, Pac-West Telecom, Forrester Research, Alcon Entertainment, Network Peripherals, Sun Microsystems, 3-Com, Lantronix, World Marketing Alliance, Pacific Bell Directories, Robert Half & Associates, Medtronix, 24-Hour Fitness, Workrite Ergonomics, Act 1 and OfficeDepot. Droubay's hallmark is his down-to-earth, genuine teaching style that delivers profound information and skills in a simple-to-apply format.

The son of a diplomat, Droubay grew up in Central and South America, speaks fluent Spanish and has traveled the world. While still in his 20s, Droubay became one of the highest-producing investment brokers in his firm nationwide. Later Anthony Robbins, the internationally renowned author, speaker and business consultant, recruited Droubay to manage and train his sales teams around the country. For eight years he was president of Anthony Robbins & Associates. He now owns Ultimate Performance, Inc., a Northern California corporate training and consulting firm, as well as Rainmaker Academy, Inc., a company that produces and markets business-training products around the world.

Droubay is also the author of, or has been a producer or consultant for, a wide range of training products and courses. They include Top Dogs: How to Run With The Big Dogs in Commercial Real Estate, Reading Genius, MGSALS, The Senior's Choice, High Impact Speaking and Coaching, Fools Gold and numerous other works. As a committed husband and father, Pete devotes much of his time to family, church and community service.

Contact:
Peter Droubay
3353 Bradshaw Road, No. 202
Sacramento, CA 95827
Phone: 800-987-1300
E-mail: droubay@aol.com
Web site: www.mgsals.com

PART II

21ST CENTURY SELLING TOOLS AND PROCESSES

CHAPTER FIVE

Living in Your Niche

Boost your industry visibility — and watch sales and profits soar —
with a message of expertise.

By Ernest F. Oriente

T he idea of living in your niche is a powerful concept. It has served as the cornerstone of our business coaching service, which has helped more than 500 clients and their companies in 11 countries. The strategy proved so successful in attracting clients to our coaching business that we began to teach our clients how to do the same for their own companies and organizations.

To understand the principles of living in your niche, you first need to answer these questions:

- Who are your best clients/prospects?
- Will it be fun to work with more of these clients/prospects?
- Can you easily find more of these clients/prospects?
- Will these clients pay full price for your products and services?
- Can you identify any painful consolidations, shifts or changes within this industry/profession?
- Can you identify any profitable trends, developments or opportunities within this industry/profession?
- How well are these clients/prospects served by your competitors within this industry/profession?
- Can you build powerful strategic alliances?

Once you've answered the above questions, you're ready to heed the principles for living in your niche. None of them is complex or difficult to follow

— they are smart, straightforward strategies for heightening industry visibility, generating clients and sharing news and information as it breaks. If you stay focused and accomplish the seven tasks outlined below, you'll boost your standing within your niche and, in turn, watch sales and profits soar.

1. WRITE INDUSTRY/PROFESSIONAL ARTICLES

A foundation for living in your niche is to write a bylined monthly article. This article is designed to position you and your company as experts within the profession of your clients and prospects. This article should be 700 to 1,000 words long, and once you get rolling, a new article will take only an hour or two to complete. Once written, it can be sent to clients and prospects by e-mail, fax or mail; inserted into a newsletter; sent to targeted industry publications; placed on Web sites; used as a foundation for training, and placed into a workbook when making a speech. You see, once you begin writing a new article each month, you can use and reuse this intellectual capital time and again.

Tip from The Coach: Have several people within your company proofread each new article to ensure accuracy, timeliness and strength of message. A word of caution: This article is not designed to be a commercial about you and your company. When you share industry knowledge, insight, trends and tips, clients and prospects will remember the expertise you provide.

2. LEVERAGE: PLACE THE ARTICLES

The next step is to have these free articles placed where your clients and prospects will read them. Some examples of where you would want to have your articles placed:

- In the publications where your client and prospects will read it
- At four or five of the most popular Web sites within an industry or profession
- As part of an industry newsletter
- Within an industry list-serve or e-zine

When your articles are placed with this kind of industry visibility, the reader (think "clients/prospects") will read what you have to share on two levels. On the first level they are going to read your articles, be impressed with what you have to share and will contact you and your company for more information (think "qualified buyers and sales"). On a second and deeper level, the people reading your articles will perceive you and your company as experts within your field, which is why your article was selected over other authors and companies (think "more sales").

Tip from The Coach: Industry and professional organizations are always seeking quality articles that will speak to their members/readers (think "clients and prospects"). Call the executive director or editor for the organization to which your clients/prospects belong, and ask for publication guidelines. In addition, ask for an editorial calendar and the preferred methods of submitting articles. Once you have this information, you can then tailor your articles and submit them for publication.

3. JOIN PROFESSIONAL COMMITTEES AND BOARDS OF DIRECTORS

Joining key industry/professional committees is another way to gain increased exposure for you and your company. This exposure adds industry/professional credibility and will allow you to boost the visibility of your products and services. Once you have participated in several committees, becoming a member of their board of directors is another invaluable part of selling in the 21st Century. As a board member, you and your company carry added clout, a high level of industry exposure and the ability to see, watch and anticipate future trends. As an added benefit, by being able to spot future trends as an industry board member, you and your company will be able to anticipate your strategic plans and provide better guidance for your clients and prospects. Plus, you can capture these future trends in your next bylined article, further leveraging the principles of living in your niche.

Tip from The Coach: Industry/professional organizations will always have a variety of committees to join. Ask the executive director where you can make the most impact and which committees will have the most clients/prospects as participants. To maximize your time and effort with these committees, attend several committee meetings before deciding which committee to join. Remember, some committees will be much more valuable than others. Find the best committees to participate in and become a significant contributor or leader.

4. HOST FREE TELECONFERENCE CALLS

Technology is making it quick, easy and cost effective to host teleconference calls for five to more than 100 participants from around the country or around the world. Invite your clients/prospects to join a free monthly teleconference call led by you and those within your company. Here are some sample topics/ideas for a teleconference call:

- The information covered in your most recent article
- An industry-specific focus group
- Pressing legal issues
- An invitation to speak with you and other board members
- New marketing ideas
- Internet trends affecting their industry/profession
- A discussion on how to increase revenue/profits
- A well-known industry author or speaker

Tip from The Coach: Industry teleconference calls are designed to be highly interactive and must honor the best principles in adult learning. To receive a list of the 30 steps/skills required before, during and after a teleconference call, send an e-mail to ernest@powerhour.com with "Teleconferencing...Train-The-Trainer" in the subject line.

5. SPEAK AT INDUSTRY/PROFESSIONAL EVENTS

Another way to live deep within your niche is to speak at trade shows, conventions and executive meetings. These are highly visible, well-attended events where you can further establish your reputation and that of your company. Honoring the principles of 21st Century Selling, you may be invited to participate as a virtual speaker/presenter via new media. In such a role, you will prepare in the same manner as you would for a traditional in-person presentation, without the time and travel to reach this event. Being a virtual presenter is an opportunity to give a number of presentations to groups of clients/prospects around the world.

Tip from The Coach: Pop quiz: Where do industry organizations find speakers? By reading the free monthly articles sent by people just like you! This is one more reason to write articles focused on the clients/prospects you most want to reach.

6. CREATE AN E-MAIL NEWSLETTER

Now is the time to create your e-mail newsletter. Why should your newsletter be sent by e-mail? Because it's a free way to stay in touch with your clients/prospects on a regular basis, and because it's easy for readers to forward your newsletter to others within their industry. And the quick delivery means you can share leading-edge information and news as it happens. Once you decide on the frequency of your newsletter, here are some examples of what to include in it:

- Your free monthly article
- An update from a recent committee meeting
- A summary of today's board of directors meeting
- An invitation to a free teleconference call
- The location, day and time of where you will be speaking in person or as a virtual presenter

See the pattern? The power of living in your niche means you can maximize the impact of your newsletter by using it to showcase the steps we discussed earlier in this chapter.

Tip from The Coach: As the foundation for attracting new coaching clients within our six niche industries/professions, we provide a free newsletter for each group of clients and prospects. As we move from newsletter to newsletter for each of these six niches, these are the minor tweaks we make:

- We change the title of the newsletter
- We change the title of the article
- We adjust the content of the article for the specific industry/profession
- We revise the author's note of each article
- We include an industry-specific e-mail signature line at the end of each newsletter

Here's the fun part. Once the newsletter is completed for our first niche, it takes fewer than 15 minutes per newsletter to make the minor tweaks for our remaining five newsletters.

7. TIE IN YOUR WEB SITE

A great deal can be said about the marketing of your Web site. For the purpose of this article, how will you answer the following questions as they relate to living in your niche?

- Does your Web site instantly speak to your clients/prospects?
- Can visitors find articles that speak to their industry/profession?
- Does your Web site mention your involvement with their industry/professional committees and their board of directors?
- Can a visitor register for your next free teleconference call?
- Can a person easily subscribe to your free newsletter?
- Will a visitor be able to review your schedule of in-person and virtual presentations?
- Does your Web site engage your clients/prospects and require specific forms of action?

Tip from The Coach: **Do you again see the pattern? A client/prospect reads your article in this month's industry magazine and then visits your Web site. There, clients see and read that you live in their world and understand the concerns and issues of their profession. As a result, they contact your company and become clients (think "sales"). Or they subscribe to your free newsletter as a result of visiting your Web site and become a prospect for the future (think "future sales").**

8. BUILD STRATEGIC ALLIANCES

Once all of the steps outlined in this article are in place, building strategic alliances is the last and most important step for living in your niche. Just to clarify, strategic alliances should include the following characteristics:

- Fun
- Easy to develop
- Flexible
- Low cost
- Win-win
- Conducive to high visibility within your niche
- Highly profitable

Here are some examples of win-win strategic alliances:

- An alliance with a book publisher within the industry of your clients/prospects
- An alliance with a non competing company that sells to the same clients/prospects you are targeting
- An alliance with a non competing e-mail newsletter that has subscribers who are your clients/prospects
- An alliance with a non competing Web site that your clients/prospects visit frequently
- An alliance with the association that serves the industry of your clients/prospects
- An alliance with a publication that your clients/prospects read
- An alliance with an influential person within this industry/profession

Tip from The Coach: **Remember, the goal of living in your niche is to be visible within the industry/profession of your clients and prospects. This means you want to select strategic-alliance partners that will add more value and increased visibility for your company/organization. In turn, you must be clear on the value and visibility you bring to your alliance partner. Think high impact and high visibility.**

Living in your niche truly is a powerful concept. After all, when you heighten your industry visibility, new clients and prospects follow. The same goes for sales and profits. And when you start spreading your message of expertise within your niche, it won't be long before you're living in it.

Ernest F. Oriente, The Coach, is founder of PowerHour®, a professional business coaching/recruiting service, and has spent (at last count!) 11,630 hours delivering customized training in leadership, traditional/Internet marketing and sales for fast-growing sales companies and entrepreneurial businesses worldwide. PowerHour® specializes in global distance learning by telephone, using a state-of-the-art conference call system for interactive and dynamic TeleForums. Biweekly TeleForums link up to 100 executives and professionals. Recent PowerHour® articles have appeared in more than 2,500 business publications and Web sites.

Contact:

Ernest Oriente

PowerHour

1402 Cutter Lane

Park City, Utah 84098

Phone: 435-615-8486

E-mail: ernest@powerhour.com; to receive a free success newsletter, e-mail Ernest@Powerhourcoachingsuccess.com

Web site: www.Powerhour.com

CHAPTER SIX

How Prospects Steal Your Brainpower

Sorry, but they want what you <u>know</u> more than
they want to do business with you.

By Dan Seidman

Megan came to one of our Executive Sales Briefings. In them, we teach entrepreneurs and sales professionals how to increase their efficiency and effectiveness in selling. Megan claimed to understand the concept of "unpaid consulting." This is the process of dumping extremely valuable insights, even complex solutions, in front of a potential client — before a relationship is established. She agreed that unpaid consulting happens, but she also believed that showing off and being thorough are big parts of designing proposals.

But now she was involved in a Big Deal and just knew we were wrong about how to prepare and present proposals.

She made a very detailed proposal on a $64 million (no kidding!) project. Her personal commission on the deal would be $3.5 million.

The people she pitched loved her proposal. In fact, they accepted it.

They just bought the stuff from someone else.

The company took apart her proposal and used it to craft the ideal solution, then began contacting companies in a lower price range than hers.

Megan will always wonder who got her $3.5-million commission check.

Postmortem: $3.5 million? When you have a great month, you might reward yourself with a gift or some extra personal time — a well-deserved trip, perhaps. How would you treat yourself after a $3.5-million bonus check? Megan never got to find out. She got suckered by a prospect who wanted to suck out her knowledge and shop her solution to someone cheaper.

Don't do what Megan did. Be very careful before creating a "work of art" proposal of high quality and detail. Get very comfortable with your potential client before investing all that time and ink. You might just write fewer proposals — and spend more pure selling time on higher probability prospects.

Proposals are the foundation of business building for most salespeople. How many of us constantly invest precious sales time to draft a proposal, pouring years of experience and expertise into this written gamble at acquiring business?

The reason most of us are so quick to accommodate potential clients is that we really do want to please people. Think of how ridiculous it would sound if you refused to provide materials to your prospect! So you and I are very likely to assume that a request for a proposal is a "yes" indicator. It reinforces our hope that we just moved one step closer to closing that sale. There is, however, the prospect's perspective. If we don't understand what might really be going on with that request, we could spend endless hours creating and delivering documents for people who have no intention of buying our products or services. Here's why.

Prospects love free consulting. They give you their biggest smile and drain your brain of all its problem-solving knowledge before you understand their true intentions. And they love it even more in print than in person. If you don't have a strategy for dealing with proposal requests, you are at the mercy of a potential client. During the past 20 years, I have analyzed many of the top sales-training organizations. It's interesting to note that virtually all of the great training systems have the wisdom to realize (and teach) how critical it is for a salesperson *not* to give everyone proposals simply because they request them.

This really is a qualifying issue. If you don't quickly sort the good prospects from the time wasters, your income can be sabotaged by bad prospects. Your expectations of who will buy from you will be inaccurate. You will lose control of the sales process. In an effort to help you understand about proposals, I offer, for the first time, my top ten list.

TOP TEN REASONS A PROSPECT
DEMANDS A PROPOSAL

(The impact to you is in parentheses.)

10. They need to keep their current vendors honest. (What a surprise — you never did have a prayer of getting the business. Many buyers simply want to monitor the market to see that they're paying a fair price. They might also use your quote to beat up their current provider and threaten to change vendors if the existing price isn't dropped — based on your proposal.)

9. They want a fair range of prices for the type of service you offer. (Thanks for the quote, but the business is going to the prospect's brother-in-law, just below your rate. Many organizations must get a specific number of quotes, regardless of their criteria for choosing a vendor. You just might be a number in a file folder, rather than a relationship being built toward a sale.)

8. They want to keep themselves up to date on the latest business processes and technologies. (Thanks for the education. Goodbye. Often buyers will monitor the marketplace to see what changes are on the horizon. Unfortunately, this has little to do with their desire to do business with you. It's safer to wait until their business peers have begun to adopt cutting-edge concepts and contraptions before risking their company's dollars on you.)

7. They think your product or service simply sounds interesting. (But they have no intention of buying! Hey, everybody loves conversation about what's going on in the marketplace. It makes those "educated" buyers appear to be experts in their field. Don't fall into the trap of believing that teaching buyers is good practice that leads to sales. Most often it is not.)

6. They need new and better ideas — to make their own changes. (Thanks for your free consulting — that really hurts, doesn't it? Ever wonder where

How Prospects Steal Your Brainpower

the term reverse-engineer came from? It's all about what's in the best inter-est of the buyer's company. Many organizations will foolishly spend more time and money re-creating your solution rather than buying it. But that's still your problem, isn't it?)

5. They just wonder how much it would cost. (Wow, you're really expen-sive! One of the biggest mistakes salespeople make is to offer price without first building a case for the need of their product. When this happens, a buyer will often make a snap decision based on your dollar figure. If you didn't know, many good negotiators even practice an expression of sur-prise at the mention of the price, just to keep you off balance.)

4. This request will get you off their back. (Oops, you forgot to qualify the prospect, didn't you? Prospects often ask for information because you've hounded them so much that they know you'll disappear — for a time — once they've been given a proposal to digest. You just need to figure out which ones are digesting your work and which ones are dumping it in the trash and hiding behind voicemail.)

3. They can look good when they pass your information to the real decision maker. (Did you spend all that time with the wrong person? Salespeople who don't have a strategy to identify the real decision maker spend too much time presenting to the wrong people. This problem will give you plen-ty of ulcers chasing the wrong contact and begging for an introduction to the right one.)

2. They honestly need their problems solved. (Too bad you don't know whom the other eight proposals are from, what they charge and maybe what they're saying about you. If you don't have competitive intelligence on who's lurking on your buyer's doorstep in the marketplace, you'll get blindsided regularly by the shock of a lost sale when a critical need exist-ed. Better start gather data on the enemy, ASAP.)

And the number one reason prospects make you pour your blood, sweat and tears into a proposal:

1. A prospect can lie to a salesperson and still get into heaven!

SALESPEOPLE, THE MOST HIGHLY PAID WRITERS IN THE WORLD

I appreciate the thinking of Tom Sant, president of the company that produces ProposalMaster, a software package that automates proposal writing. He claims that salespeople are among the most highly paid writers in the world. When you calculate the time invested in designing proposals and measure that against a rep's quota, you could get a figure in the hundreds, even thousands, of dollars per hour. No one, except maybe Stephen King or John Grisham, is making that kind of money writing.

Preparing proposals often offers false hopes to the most experienced sales pro. This person really believes that everyone asking for a customized, written solution is *ready to buy.*

Please, please stop wasting your time jumping through hoops to design proposals for everyone who nods his or her head or grunts into your telephone. Qualify first, then begin to work with your best potential clients. Your organization should have some criteria for what defines a good prospect. Use it or immediately create your own in order to save yourself from sales heartbreak. One good strategy might be to charge a fee for a proposal. Obviously, a prospect who is not serious will not pay for it. If this works for you, implement it. Your organization, however, might not choose this strategy. So get a grip on what looks like a realistic buyer and craft your plan without giving away all of your solutions.

The lesson here is that you need to set some guidelines to determine which prospects are worth the investment of your time in proposal design. Otherwise, you'll waste a lot of that time showboating in print for prospects who have no intention of doing business with you. If you don't kill the weeds, you'll have very little time to find, pick and smell the flowers.

Dan Seidman has been involved in high-impact sales and marketing for privately run companies since 1980. He is an early adopter of the Internet, selling for the first Internet job site, Online Career Center, in 1993. Seidman took his extensive sales-management and training expertise online in '99. He currently manages the widely publicized Web site of selling disasters,

How Prospects Steal Your Brainpower

www.SalesAutopsy.com. Sales & Marketing Management Magazine calls the site "a cult hit among sales folks." Seidman invests his business life in speaking to entrepreneurs, sales professionals and executives about these amusing, lesson-filled sales horror stories. The best and worst of these selling disasters have been compiled in his new book, The Death of 20th Century Selling. On the personal side, Dan enjoys scuba diving and competes in World Master's Sports, where he is a two-time gold medalist in basketball, playing on a U.S. team. He also volunteers on the Web advisory board for Willow Creek Association, serves on the board of Sales and Marketing Executives of Chicago and edits the e-zine of the Small Publishers Association of North America.

Dan Seidman

SalesAutopsy.com

190 E. Dundee Road

Barrington, IL 60010

Phone: 847-359-7860

E-mail: dan@salesautopsy.com

Web site: www.salesautopsy.com.

CHAPTER SEVEN

The E-mail Advantage

Sure, electronic communication is fast and efficient.
But do you know how to make the most of it?

By Auren Hoffman

S alespeople who can effectively use e-mail as a communications medium
can be much more productive. Although e-mail is a staple of every
salesperson's pitch, it is rarely used to its maximum effectiveness. In this
chapter, we'll examine the power of e-mail and provide tips on how to write
your e-mails in order to achieve their maximum effectiveness.

Why is e-mail so powerful? Let's consider its many crucial advantages:

Time dimensions are different today.

People move much faster in today's world. They want documents fast (no
waiting for FedEx) and in soft copy so they can edit them. They want
variable-pricing models (spreadsheet models that can calculate their price or
their ROI given different sets of data). They want handy information at their
fingertips. And they want it all now.

It's easier to return e-mails than voice mails.

Voice mails rarely get returned. Why? Often it is because the target isn't interested in the voice mail, but more often it is because voicemails take a lot of
effort to return. The target needs to get a pen, write down the phone number
and the name, and then actively call the person trying to sell them. And making calls takes time — time that a target might not want to give up in the
opening stages of a sale. E-mails, on the other hand, are very easy to return.

It's easier to forward e-mails than voice mails.

Forwarding e-mails is simple — people do it all the time. Forwarding voice mails is more complex, takes more time, and can be more difficult (especially when you are away from the office and forget the extension of a colleague).

If people are not interested, they will usually tell you faster via e-mail.

Often, when I'm selling for BridgePath, I'll get a response via e-mail saying, "This looks great, but we do not have a budget to buy your product for six months." That response allows me to concentrate on higher-probability prospects. I never get my voice-mails returned with a "no thanks" — I usually just get silence.

It is a good intro to put prospects on your monthly/quarterly newsletter.

If you do not have a regular newsletter that highlights your wins to your prospects, create one. (I would suggest monthly or quarterly.) You can easily send your newsletter via e-mail. (You'd be surprised how many people read the BridgePath Executive Letter.) If you send a prospect an introductory e-mail, be sure to let the prospect know that you are going to add her to your regular newsletter distribution.

E-mail can reach the target easier.

E-mail rarely has gates. In fact, I have never had a sales target who didn't read his or her own e-mail. There are only a few CEOs who have their secretaries screen their e-mails. I see e-mail as the great equalizer. When I was in college, I started an e-mail conversation with Steve Ballmer (now the CEO of Microsoft) because I sent him an e-mail he found useful. When a starving college student can communicate with a billionaire at 2 a.m., you know you have a powerful medium.

E-mail addresses are easy to figure out.

I always tell the salespeople at BridgePath that if you can't figure out the e-mail of a prospect, you don't deserve to get the sale. There are only so many permutations of e-mail addresses — and often if you know one e-mail, you know all the others in the company. Also, you can call the front desk and ask for a prospect's e-mail address – they are more likely to give it to you than someone's direct dial.

Funny story: a friend of mine attended an inspiring speech by a CEO at a hot technology company. That night, my friend sent an e-mail to the CEO with his résumé saying how much he'd like to work for the company. But my friend did not know the CEO's e-mail address. So what did he do? He sent five e-mails to five different addresses — firstname.lastname@company.com, firstname@company.com, lastname@company.com, flastname@company.com, firstnamel@company.com — hoping that one would get through.

The next morning my friend received an e-mail from the CEO: "Hey, I got all five of your e-mails. You must really want to work here. Let's schedule an interview for tomorrow." Sure enough, two weeks later, my friend was working for the new company.

Update all the "influencers" where you are in the process — not just today's target.

Often when you are making a complex enterprise-wide sale, as we do at BridgePath, you have many different influencers and decision makers. In the old way of selling you'd move around the organization and go back and forth and get buy-in from each decision maker in series. Today, e-mail makes it much easier to work in parallel.

When I make a sale, I'm usually successful because at least once every two weeks I've sent a personalized e-mail updating everyone in the organization where we are in the process. You'd be surprised how seldom people communicate within a company. People are frequently really appreciative when they get e-mails from me saying, "Just wanted to let you know that I met today with <your CEO's name here>, who had these thoughts about BridgePath…"

Attached documents make negotiating contracts faster.

E-mail is the new way to negotiate contracts. Instead of faxing back and forth to one another contracts with handwriting, you can send an attached document quickly and easily. Programs such as MS Word and Word Perfect allow you to track your changes (in Word go to the Tools/Track Changes menu) as you go forward. And if you are afraid your target might try to make untracked changes, you can do a document compare each time you get a marked-up version.

Given all these advantages, you'll still be making lots of phone calls, sending letters, scanning faxes and doing visits. You don't get out of hard work just because you use e-mail. But e-mail is going to make all the other parts of your job easier.

TIPS FOR USING E-MAIL

Writing good e-mails is really, really hard. Writing bad e-mails is really easy. Follow the tips below to get maximum results from your e-mails.

Always remember that all e-mails can easily be forwarded.

Write the e-mail in a way that makes sense to someone who does not know you. Put things in context, spell out acronyms and refer to people with both first and last names. Even if you've developed a great relationship with someone, find a way to be both friendly and professional via e-mail.

Spell-check and proofread e-mails before sending.

People have a tendency to have many unprofessional errors in e-mails because it is a quick medium. Grammatical and spelling mistakes are extremely common. Do not fall into that trap.

Copy the person who gave you the introduction.

If the executive vice president asks you to talk to a specific person lower down in the organization, copy the EVP when you send the introductory e-mail.

This does two things:

- It keeps the EVP in the loop. Because the EVP will probably be a key future decision maker, you want to ensure that person is aware of what you are doing.
- It legitimizes you to the target. You really did get an intro from the EVP – and you are proving it by the CC.

Write a catchy subject line.

The subject line is the most important part of the e-mail for a few reasons:

- Many e-mails don't get read. You need something catchy to get it read.
- The e-mail might get forwarded to someone else, and you want that person to read it.
- E-mail subjects tend to live on for a long time because e-mail communication is generally in "reply" mode – meaning I send you an e-mail, you reply to me and then I reply back to you. All with the same continuing subject.

You'll never see a BridgePath salesperson write "BridgePath" as the subject line. That's the easy thing to write, but it is not the most effective.

Rework your "From" address.

Most people's "from" address just consists of their first and last names. But you might be able to convey more information in the "from" field — which is generally the most read part of your e-mail. All my e-mails come from "Auren Hoffman (BridgePath)" rather than just "Auren Hoffman." I know some people who add the one word that defines their product to the "from" field. But you have to be careful—too much of a slick message will make your e-mail look like spam.

Keep it short.

Long e-mails don't get read. Most people don't realize this, so I'll repeat myself: long e-mails don't get read! So don't write long e-mails. It is much harder to say what you have to say in a few sentences, but your messages will be much more effective if you can master a shorter message.

All paragraphs should be less than four lines long—and use bullet points whenever possible.

This is a rule — don't break it. People tend to skip over things they read on the screen. So make reading easy for people. They are probably not going to print out the e-mail (unless it is a newsletter), so be sure to write for the screen medium.

The "P.S." is the most important part of the e-mail body.

When you are sending an e-mail and you want to stress something, be sure to include a "P.S." A "P.S." is generally the most read part of any e-mail. People will skip over a long body but they will almost always, instinctively, look at the postscript.

Use this to your advantage by adding one to two sentences at the end of your message recapping what you said or discussing a new point of interest that you want your reader to look at. Some skilled letter writers will refer back to the middle of a letter to encourage readers to review the document in detail. I usually put the call to action in my postscript.

I'm not totally keen on the "P.P.S.," though. Sometimes that's overkill. But I've seen the post-postscript used effectively when it is combined with humor.

If you send an attachment, tell people how long it will take to read it.

When I send attachments, I'll usually accompany them with this message: "Please review the attached document. It should take you about 12 minutes to read over." Giving your prospects a reasonable time frame to review a document shows them that you respect their time. It also allows them to plan to read it accordingly. Most busy people who get attachments will file the attachment away and forget to read it.

Watch for formatting issues — use simple text that translates well into any e-mail system.

If you are writing an e-mail in MS Outlook, remember that the formatting options available to you are not available to many others who receive e-mails. So try to write the e-mails in plain text. Use a "*" rather than a formatted bullet. And watch for funny symbols, different font use, color use, or curly or "smart" quotes.

Keep the signature relevant — don't put your title unless it helps.

If you are sending a sales-related e-mail, you don't have to tell people you're a sales manager. Unless you are a VP or above, titles usually don't help secure the prospect.

Attach a vCard.

I find it very useful when people send me a vCard with their e-mail. A vCard (usually a .vcf file) is an attached contact file that is compatible with many contact management systems such as MS Outlook and Lotus cc:Mail. vCards carry contact info, and you can also have them carry a marketing message and information about your product.

I personally don't use vCards, but they can be helpful tools for sales representatives.

Auren Hoffman is CEO of BridgePath, an online competitor-to-competitor marketplace bringing temporary and permanent staffing firms together to create collaborative placement transactions. Hoffman previously co-founded Kyber Systems, an intranet development firm, where he managed the implementation of intranet and extranet systems for Bain & Company, Sybase, Charles Schwab, ASUS, EventSource and BizNet. He is an active participant in the Technology Network, a term member of the Council on Foreign Relations and the founder of the Silicon Forum. George magazine named him one of six future leaders in December 1999, and VAR Business named him one of the top 30 entrepreneurs under 30 in December 2000. Hoffman holds a B.S.E. in industrial engineering and operations research from the University of California, Berkeley. Hoffman also writes a monthly column called Summation (www.summation.net), detailing his philosophy on business, policy and life.

Contact:

BridgePath

Address: 463 Bryant St, 2nd Floor, San Francisco, CA 94107

E-mail: hoffman@bridgepath.com

Web site: www.bridgepath.com

CHAPTER EIGHT

The Quest for Customers

How a company acquires new business is rarely documented and seldom understood – even though it is arguably the most important function of any firm.

By Martyn R. Lewis

O f all the assets in today's enterprises, none is as valuable as a new customer. Peter Drucker said, "There is only one valid definition of business purpose: *To create a customer.*"[1] And despite the ebb and flow of business trends and dire warnings of the extinction of the salesperson, the responsibility of creating a new customer still belongs to the sales professional.

Certainly, changes to the traditional role of salespeople have altered the way they will face 21st Century Selling. In addressing these issues, we will look at two allied sales-related methodologies: Customer Relationship Management (CRM), already firmly entrenched in the market, and the emerging field called Customer Acquisition Management (CAM).

Its rapid success has established CRM as a full-fledged phenomenon. *Business Week* expects this sector to increase at more than 50 percent annually and to become an $11.6 billion market by 2003. Some confusion, however, surrounds CRM. Jim Dickie of the Insight Technology Group finds two-thirds of all CRM implementations have fallen short of expectations. This is probably because CRM's strength is its ability to understand and analyze an organization's *current* customers. CRM's value to a salesperson seeking new customers may be negligible, but to be fair, that is not the job it was designed to do. But while many companies might feel pressured to institute large and expensive customer relationship management systems, maybe what they really want is just a few more customers.

[1]Peter Drucker – Management: Tasks, Responsibilities, Practices, 1973

Customer Acquisition Management addresses that desire, focusing on the task of finding new business. It has the ability to lead sales professionals through the labyrinth of a complex business-to-business (B2B) sales cycle and to determine the best route to the close. CAM poses crucial questions: who are the potential customers, where are they, and from whom and why do they currently buy? It deals with the issue of new leads, how to approach them and with what value proposition. It enables the user to encompass all resources in the organization that have input in the sales function. Most importantly, it addresses the current situations and prevailing mindsets found in many of today's B2B enterprise organizations. That last point may not sound like a lot until we look more closely.

THE BIG MISCONCEPTION

Major international organizations, mid-sized companies and startups alike rarely document and seldom understand the customer acquisition process — even though it is arguably the most important function of any company. Even more troubling, many people inside and outside these organizations have serious misconceptions about the best ways to get new customers. If we tried to document the flawed strategy, it might look like this.

The Step	The Misconception
#1 Lead Generation	The organization invests in a number of marketing initiatives, from advertising to direct mail, trade shows and now the corporate Web site. From these efforts, a number of targeted decision makers will contact us for more information.
#2 Sales Presentation	Leads are passed to the salespeople so they can meet with prospects to give them the company message. The salesperson will deliver a carefully crafted presentation on the company, its products, its value propositions and glowing customer testimonials.

#3 Proposal and Order	The salesperson will document the solution using a proven proposal format. This is presented to the prospect, along with an accompanying ROI analysis. The salesperson gets the prospect's commitment by way of a signed contract or order.
#4 Objection Handling and Negotiation	If the prospect still hasn't said yes, the salesperson will use various powers of persuasion to handle objections and gain the commitment. He or she will use an arsenal of sales skills to develop a relationship with the prospect and thereby close the deal.

Perhaps you think that I'm painting this picture with too broad a brush. Unfortunately, we have found that this "default" sales cycle too often reflects the thoughts of many individuals, from the mailroom to the boardroom and everywhere from startups to multinationals – including many salespeople. Worse yet, the underlying and prevailing behavior of many organizations only reinforces this misconception. Amazingly, many organizations seem to believe their customers behave differently in their buying habits than they do themselves. Consider the following example.

A CASE STUDY

To understand how sales professionals get new business, consider how your company would approach the purchase of a big-ticket product or service, one that your company is not currently considering purchasing and that comes from a company that you have never dealt with. In other words, welcome to the real world of sales.

Now let's consider how your company would react to a sales call or perhaps direct mail for a new software application that would supposedly pay for itself in fewer than 18 months. How quickly would you respond? Would you respond at all? Who would respond, and who would have the authority to evaluate a possible purchase? Who else would investigate and evaluate alternatives, and who would ultimately decide to place the order? How long would this take? Where would the funds come from, and who would have to approve this? What decision criteria would you use in deciding to invest? And let's not forget some of the more complex questions: What political agendas in your company could influence the purchase process and timing? Who in your organization would support or oppose the decision? Would everybody in your company have the same answers to these questions, or would they differ in some way? If so, how?

These are just some of the factors that companies expect their salespeople not only to know but also to influence in the prospect organization. Yet many of them might find it difficult to describe how major purchasing decisions work in their companies. In fact, in many cases, we see that the most successful salespeople become more familiar with the client organization than those who work there.

If we think back to that "default" sales cycle and its misconceptions, how far would that salesperson get knocking on *your* door?

WHAT'S REALLY GOING ON

We've done some serious digging in many organizations. We often find many unfulfilled expectations, along with surprisingly little knowledge of how salespeople actually use their time. Even senior managers with years of business experience often do not fully realize what is going on in their sales organizations. Here are the twelve most common misconceptions and unfulfilled expectations that we have found.

1. New customer acquisition cycle is often three to four times longer than expectations.
2. Number of leads required to generate an order is as much as five times higher than planned.
3. New salesperson ramp-up time is often two to three times longer than anticipated.
4. Actual productive selling time is often only 60 to 75 percent of what had been previously assumed.
5. Salespeople have lots of seemingly necessary non-selling things to do.

6. Many successful salespeople cannot always define the specifics that lead to their success.

7. The time that sales managers spend getting information for pipeline management, forecasting, etc., often results in poor quality information and sometimes in no information at all.

8. Forecasting is often based on unrealistic optimism, fear or historic run-rates.

9. Market trends are often not detected until they impact revenue, even though signs may have been apparent months earlier.

10. Great product offerings do not automatically translate into new business.

11. A successful sale depends more on listening and coordinating than on presenting and persuading.

12. Many organizations are still challenged to complete the transition to a solution-selling model.

An illuminating picture, and all the more reason to realize the extent of a major selling crisis that exists in today's B2B marketplace. It is also significant to note that many struggling or failing companies do or did not lack for good products, experienced management teams and dedicated, hard-working employees. Many promising startups had, at least to start with, the necessary funding and yet still failed. And ironically, many struggling companies also have (or sadly <u>had</u>) a fiercely loyal customer base. For example, Digital Equipment had tens of thousands of loyal customers, but that was not enough to save the company.

The one thing that all of these companies had in common was *their inability to attract new customers.*

THE SELLING CRISIS

The current selling crisis has five root causes, explained below and followed by a brief comment on how to resolve or mitigate each one.

1. The purchasing procedures of companies have changed significantly during the past half-dozen years. In the empowered and networked organization, finding the buyer or decision maker has become difficult, as many more "influencers" and advisors are now involved in the process.

The new methods of purchasing are with us for the foreseeable future, and besides, we can't exercise much control over how our prospects are conducting their purchase processes.

2. Technology, especially the Internet, has had a dramatic impact on the sales organization. The salesperson is no longer the single pipeline of information between the company and its prospects. Gone are the days when the customer relied on the salesperson to provide product information, or when the salesperson could actually make a good living just by delivering and even controlling that flow of information. Technology has now released many sales professionals from such duties as order administration, proposal preparation, configuration and pricing, and they now must concentrate solely on the primary mission of identifying leads and transforming them into satisfied and profitable customers.

The rate of change and adoption of technology is hardly going to slow, and we can expect that these factors will only continue to impact the sales organization.

3. Due to increased pressure to raise productivity and meet shareholder expectations, organizations have to demand more from their sales forces. There is the usual quest for greater productivity and higher yields, but there are also other demands that we have seen increase. The sales forecast is no longer just a way to see what each sales person is doing – it has become a critical factor in managing the overall supply chain, and in many publicly owned corporations it influences stock-market valuations and activity. Salespeople also need to coordinate and leverage far more internal and partner resources than ever before.

Companies are not going to ease up on the demands they are placing on their sales organizations. In fact, we fully expect that the cry of "more with less" will only become louder during the next few years.

4. Product cycles are getting increasingly shorter. Because many conventional selling styles are based on osmosis, history and other informal means, the sales force has less time than ever to learn the successful selling formula required for the new product.

The speed at which products can be brought to market, and the encroachment rate of obsolescence, will only increase.

5. A definable sales process does not exist in most sales organizations, despite what they might say or believe. Let me offer my definition of the sales process:

The sales process is the documented sequence of events that, like a roadmap, leads the selling team through the process of developing a raw lead into a satisfied and profitable customer.

Here is the only one of the five factors about which we can do something. This area can contribute the single largest gain in results for the vast majority of today's enterprise sales forces.

THE BENEFITS OF PROCESS

Let me make here what I believe to be the most important point in this whole discussion.

If you expect to succeed in today's arena of complex B2B sales, you cannot engage that marketplace with anything less than a totally engineered and scientific approach.

And we are neither the first ones nor the only ones to talk about this.

D. Forbes Ley[2] outlines the complexity of sales. "When you consider the many facets the salesperson must control, from the ferreting out of prospects through to a successful close, you have to conclude the subject of selling is somewhat overwhelming."

Miller-Heiman[3] points out, "The hit-and-miss pitch techniques that were the mainstay of selling in calmer years can't even begin to address … sales in today's super-heated markets."

[2]D. Forbes Ley – The Best Seller, 1984
[3]Miller-Heiman – Strategic Selling, 1985

The evidence points to numerous benefits to organizations when they design, implement and manage an optimal sales process:

- **Integration of existing technologies, practices, and methodologies**
- **Shorter sales cycles**
- **Greater forecast accuracy**
- **Faster detection and response to market trends**
- **Faster ramp-up time for new sales hires**
- **Sales skills and performance needs and analysis**
- **Massively increased sales productivity**
- **Aligned and coordinated internal and partner resources**
- **Increased, predictable revenue**
- **Decreased costs**
- **Full utilization of CRM**
- **Transition to true solution selling**

CONCLUSION

Considering the continual friction of people vs. process, artist vs. techie, it may seem almost paradoxical that salespeople and sales organizations would thrive on an engineered sales process. But a growing body of evidence strongly suggests that when designed and implemented in a responsible manner, the application of process to the activities of the sales organization will yield remarkable results.

And this is not as revolutionary or bleeding-edge as it may sound. Consider what William Penn said in 1693. "Method goes far to prevent trouble in business, for it makes the task easy, hinders confusion, saves abundance of time and instructs those that have business depending both what to do and what to hope."[4] And indeed what sales professional wouldn't want to make the job easier, get rid of confusion, save time, and have a clearer idea of what has to get done and what to expect from the effort?

For too long, too many companies have viewed sales as a mysterious "black box." They have poured endless resources into the box, trained and retrained the sales force, changed commission structures and initiatives aimed at gaining more output from the sales team. However, real success will come

[4]William Penn (1644–1718) - Some Fruits of Solitude, 1693

only to those who take the lid off the box and start to understand the mechanisms of the sales engine inside. They can then design, implement, measure, manage and optimize a first-class and world-class sales operation. In today's highly competitive world, we know that even the best mousetrap can die in the marketplace without an effective sales and marketing effort. For those organizations engaged in complex B2B selling, their very livelihoods will depend on their ability to build and maintain high-performance sales organizations through the design, implementation and management of their optimal sales process.

Martyn Lewis began his career in the United Kingdom where he successfully worked in the technical management of large software-development projects. In 1982, he joined Digital Equipment of Canada and his eleven-year career with DEC spanned a variety of sales, marketing and executive positions culminating in the position of VP of marketing and sales operations. In 1993, Martyn left Digital to become president and CEO of Drake International, where he oversaw the reversal of a multi-year decline in revenue to achieve growth in excess of three times that of the market.

Martyn left Drake in 1995 to found Market-Partners in Toronto, where he developed the company's core philosophy, The Science of Sales & Marketing, a process-driven sales productivity methodology, accessible to clients in both consultative and system format. The company expanded to San Jose, CA, and includes clients such as Novell, PeopleSoft and Oracle as well as many smaller companies.

Martyn is a frequent spokesman for the industry and is a regular contributor to various industry newsletters. He is also a highly respected speaker and seminar leader and conducts workshops across North America. He has been a keynote speaker at industry events including Comdex, the Association for the Advancement of Relationship Marketing and the American Marketing Association.

In his spare time he has directed his passion for flying into being an advisor and active pilot for Youth Flight, a charity organization dedicated to enabling underprivileged and challenged children to realize the dream of flight.

Contact:

Martyn R. Lewis

President and CEO

Market-Partners

2660 John Montgomery Drive, #27,

San Jose, CA, 95148,

Phone: 408-251-5100

Fax: 603-676-8992

mlewis@market-partners.com,

www.market-partners.com

CHAPTER NINE

SFA or Sorry?

When sales software does more harm than good, you have to help it deliver.

By Scott Bonds

Entering the 21st Century, the dot-com boom and bust affirmed what most of us already knew: technology can be a wonderful tool, but businesses succeed only when they make sales and deliver what customers want. Nevertheless, many executives continue in their quest for the technological silver bullet that will transform their sales force into the powerhouse they imagine.

Sadly, there is no such silver bullet that will kill anything other than your budget. Successful sales organizations are made of talented people who not only are equipped with an effective sales pipeline process but also work together on a well-thought-out strategy. Without a solid foundation, technology is little help to your organization.

But even with that foundation, technology can be a blessing or a curse — too often a curse. Have you ever been asked to use a new software package that was supposed to help your company, only to find that tasks took longer to accomplish? Have you ever bought a system based on its promising features and client references, only to find that you didn't receive the same benefits at your company?

Sales software, commonly known as Sales Force Automation systems, or SFA, is no exception. In fact, many companies have invested millions of dollars to buy and maintain their SFA systems, but they have only been able to use the programs effectively as costly contact-management systems — not to make more sales.

This chapter will examine the pitfalls of popular SFA systems. If the information convinces you not to spend hundreds of thousands of dollars on an SFA system that doesn't deliver, this will have been a worthwhile lesson. Better yet, we'll look at ways beyond SFA to help you build upon your solid sales foundation, save your salespeople time and make well-informed strategy decisions.

WHAT WENT WRONG WITH SFA?

Many of the SFA systems and Customer Relationship Management (CRM) systems available today were built with senior executives in mind. (CRM, a complementary tool to SFA, performs many similar functions for managing customer information. Some CRM systems contain SFA functions and include other capabilities geared toward customer service, customer relations and other areas not directly sales related.) By offering components such as forecasting and pipeline management, which includes targeting prospects and estimating the value of pending sales, SFA's tools are designed to appeal to the people who decide whether to buy the systems for their company. Although the features are promising, SFA systems haven't enabled more thorough forecasts because salespeople, under pressure to perform and pressed for time to enter information, sometimes do not give high priority to the accuracy of the data. As a result, executives have not been able to manage their pipeline more effectively. Ultimately, many SFA systems become time-consuming and costly contact-management tools.

WHAT DIDN'T WORK

Kyber Systems is a large (fictional) company using SFA. Kyber spent millions, customized the program to its existing sales process, and then changed its process to take advantage of the new system where it made sense. The system is feature rich, one of the largest and most reputable SFA packages available. The deployment was unusually smooth. But Kyber isn't seeing the results it had hoped for.

Management overlooked a built-in conflict for salespeople. The system takes the salesperson's time to populate the database — time that a staff paid on commission would rather spend selling. The sales manager, though, needs the information to make forecasts and to evaluate and support the salespeople. To keep the boss happy, the salespeople have been doing the minimum to get by, and consequently the data is lacking. They use the system to manage their contacts, but they fail to update pipeline and forecasting data thoroughly. The data they input is quite often inaccurate. In turn, the forecast the sales manager generates is flawed, leading to poor decisions. Then the manager goes directly to the salespeople to get a better feel for their activities and passes on a manual estimate to the VP of sales after hours of meetings with his staff — a step the SFA vendor had promised to make obsolete.

Saction is a medium-sized (fictional) company with an SFA system that is not the largest available, but a good one in management's estimation. Although management couldn't afford too much customization, it is able to track sales efforts and generate data. The sales force is fairly comfortable with the tool because they can keep track of leads in one place. But, wary of making it too easy for management to bother them about leads, the salespeople try to limit their entries to what will put them in the best light and will lead to acceptable forecasts. That way, they can avoid a discussion with their boss and focus on hitting their numbers. This leaves the boss thinking prospects are better than they are, making it difficult to decide when to jump in to help reorient a salesperson's efforts or to reassess the company's overall sales strategy as the market changes.

A.H. Tanger and Associates is a small (also fictional) company that uses spreadsheets, e-mail and contact management software to manage its pipeline. The firm's small sales team is uncertain of the SFA system's potential benefits. One problem is that the sales team has lost contact info and has had someone call an account more than once for the same thing. Furthermore, the team's projections lack accuracy. They don't have much insight into the sales pipeline — the salespeople don't know for certain whether they should focus on improving their phone scripts, or if objections are slowing them down, or if their advertising has been helping. They go by gut feelings because the metrics, which should tell them what is happening in a dispassionate, unbiased manner, are simply unavailable. This prevents them from noticing changes to their pipeline against past pipelines and limits their decision-making ability. Instead of relying on information entered into an SFA system, the sales manager spends time meeting with each person to review progress and asks the salespeople to keep records with whatever means they are comfortable. When salespeople leave, it can be difficult to transfer their leads to someone else.

WHY IT DIDN'T WORK

The problem in each of these examples is that SFA has done a better job aligning with sales management than with salespeople. After all, executives buy the software; so SFA providers create features to entice the top brass. The fundamental variable affecting the utility of the SFA tool is the quality of the information populating it. If salespeople do not contribute quality information to the system, the forecasts and reports it produces will lead to bad decisions.

The misalignment comes from the way in which SFA vendors design their systems, how sales management asks salespeople to participate, and what truly motivates salespeople. SFA applications are generally designed to enable the tracking of sales opportunities through the pipeline. The salesperson is asked to enter information throughout the process about the nature of a lead, contact information, pipeline status, activities they have done related to the lead, next steps, etc. Most of the information they are asked to input is more useful to their boss in managing the sales team than it is to the salesperson. Salespeople are hired, fired and compensated on their ability to make sales. It's what they want to do.

Therein lies the dilemma. The salesperson must enter certain information to please the boss, who wishes to use the SFA tool to manage the pipeline, forecast sales, manage the sales force, examine what parts of the pipeline call for a new strategy, etc. If the salesperson accurately enters all the requested information, the boss is happy. But it takes the staff considerable time that could otherwise be spent making sales. At the same time, "full disclosure" makes it easier for the company to replace the salesperson because all sales leads are fully documented.

If, on the other hand, the salespeople enter optimistic and minimal information about leads (to satisfy the boss's requirement to enter information into the system), they reduce the amount of time spent on SFA and do not provide enough information to enable the company to replace them. The salespeople also can make the forecast look good enough to keep the manager off their backs even when things are slow.

Gathering quality information is a hurdle. Maybe you can figure out how to do it; maybe you can't. If you're at a loss, don't waste your money on a system that requires you solve the information-gathering puzzle before you can reap the system's benefits. Instead of buying an SFA program with attractive but ineffective features, put together a more affordable system that has fewer bells and whistles but makes both salespeople and management more effective. It's more important that you understand how your people work and how to generate and support more business, rather than throwing an abundance of expensive features at your sales challenge and hoping the technology will solve it for you.

SFA FOR THE SALESPEOPLE

One of the best ways to make sales teams more effective is to help them streamline their day-to-day tasks and give them greater visibility into their prospects and accounts so the teams may serve them better. Pipeline visibility isn't just for managers — salespeople can make more sales when they are able to see what industries their style has been most successful with, or where they have been having more trouble advancing the sales process compared to their colleagues, or how accurate their sales-cycle expectations have proved to be.

Salespeople want to sell more. If you give them tools that they understand and that help them succeed, they will provide your management with better, more accurate and more frequently updated information. Equipped with high-quality information from their sales force, managers are able to make more accurate projections, adjust their sales strategies and help their salespeople target their efforts more productively. Also, communicating your commitment to helping salespeople succeed – not with top-down decisions but with bottom-up support – will engender the sort of environment that leads to dedicated salespeople who work hard to perform when management is their ally.

BUILDING THE SYSTEM

Start by understanding how your company and its individual salespeople sell. Compare the approach of your best performers, and note how they interact with your sales process and pipeline. Examine the accuracy of your forecasts and how your salespeople are using your existing tools, such as ACT, MS Outlook, Lotus Notes or an assortment of forms. Look at what works, what doesn't, and examine where your salespeople are spending their time. Involving salespeople throughout the process is a crucial component of this approach.

Then analyze how technology actually helps with sales. Determine whether the features of currently available SFA systems would help your salespeople save time and build better relationships with prospects and accounts. Setting aside your knowledge of the technology for a moment, envision your ideal SFA solution. Consider first how this system would help your salespeople *quickly increase* their sales and commissions.

Could your salespeople be spending less time looking up information on prospects and more time on the phone? If they could quickly search through reference stories by industry, would it help them make more effective calls?

If you want a successful SFA solution, make sure the system is designed with the salespeople in mind. When salespeople use SFA the right way, with management's support and open dialogue, you'll build upon a solid sales foundation, save the salespeople time and make well-informed strategy decisions. In such a setting, technology will work with, not against, your salespeople and your company.

Scott Bonds is president of the technology consulting firm, Bonds Consulting, Berkeley, California.

The firm employs technology leaders who understand the importance of strong communication and collaboration between business leaders and technology specialists in making profitable strategic technology decisions.

Before starting Bonds Consulting, Bonds co-founded BridgePath, a recruiting exchange, and consulted for companies including Charles Schwab, Disney, Microsoft and Siemens. He has a degree in electrical engineering and computer science with a minor in business administration from University of California, Berkeley.

Contact:

Bonds Consulting

2342 Shattuck Avenue, Suite 107

Berkeley, CA 94704

Phone: 415-412-1621

E-mail: scott@bondsc.com

PART III

GETTING IT DONE IN THE 21ST CENTURY

CHAPTER TEN

Loyalty Breeds Success

Sales relationships often benefit from a woman's touch.
But everyone can learn about customer interaction and satisfaction.

By Sandra Swanson

I n my first job, with Xerox, I witnessed the best and worst of sales presentations. As a systems analyst who supported sales representatives, I learned how the top salespeople, many of them women, trusted their instincts and then perfected their unique sales styles.

After two years in the position, I knew I could be successful in sales by listening to and supporting the customer. In the first year of my sales career, I survived on my instincts, particularly my instincts as a woman, to detect and display emotions, to organize and pay attention to detail, and to persevere.

In 21st Century Selling, women need to be aware of their female senses and use them to their advantage. Women excel in diplomacy and a non-threatening communication style that not only is effective with all levels of management but also can provide them with an edge in sales. Another valuable asset is the ability to listen — to respond by smiling and giving verbal feedback and nodding. As a sales manager, I constantly reminded my team to ask questions and listen. In turn, customers will tell you everything you need to know to sell them. Anyone can take a few cues to adjust a sales style to become more in tune with customers.

In keeping with the themes of listening and responding to an individual's needs, I've come up with four strategies for sales success. With them, you'll connect with customers, work more effectively in group situations, build relationships and pay attention to detail. All will give you an edge over the competition.

MAKE A PERSONAL CONNECTION

Like everyone, I had a customer who tested my sales skills. He was content with his current vendor and saw no need to switch to our product, even though he agreed it had its advantages. My competition had done a good job of building customer loyalty. The challenge kept me awake at night because I knew that my product was a better fit for this customer and more cost effective.

One day I remembered all the novelties that I had seen in his office and recalled comments he had made about his personal tastes. Trusting my instincts, I began strategizing. I bought a replica of the hand in the box that appeared in the movie *The Hand*, a takeoff from the Munsters. I inscribed on the hand, "Hands Down RELCON meets your needs." The hand was battery operated, and the fingers moved. So, when I had his secretary take it into his office, the hand began to wave as he opened the box. He laughed and subsequently became one of my most loyal customers. The lesson: by paying attention to personal information about my customer, I was able to connect and close the sale.

WORK WELL WITH OTHERS

Multitasking, organizing and following up are additional strengths of women. Salespeople who make promises and do not fulfill them annoy customers. It's important to prioritize, organize and take care of multiple customers with ease.

In sales, more than one decision maker is usually involved in the process. In my sales career with Xerox, I represented a very expensive product with a lengthy sales cycle, which required the approval of many department heads. In one account I had approval from the decision maker to proceed only if his entire staff approved as well. I had to be patient and make sure that I balanced everyone's needs in order to reach a consensus to move forward with the purchase.

In another sales situation, a decision maker shared his frustration with me about his staff's weak performance. I quickly recognized the opportunity and volunteered personally to conduct training on closing techniques. By demonstrating my commitment to him in going beyond normal expectations, I earned loyalty from him and his staff.

Women excel at building and maintaining relationships, which contributes to their success in sales and management. They encourage interactive involvement and know how to be sensitive to all the personalities in a group.

BUILD CUSTOMER RELATIONSHIPS

Too often the personal touch takes a backseat to technology, but now it seems to be making a resurgence in the marketplace. Examples are never forgetting birthdays, sending thank-you notes and remembering baby gifts. Companies involved with e-commerce have learned that their customers insist on some level of live interaction during their transactions. Direct-mail companies such as Gateway Computer have opened retail stores to help answer their customers' questions. Costco calls customers to be sure their needs have been met and that their orders have been processed in a timely manner.

Sometimes customers appreciate the simple gestures most. I remember one who told me that no one, not even his family, remembered his birthday one year except me. He never forgot my effort and rewarded my gesture with loyalty.

Although our profession has evolved from library research on customers and individual typewritten proposals to Internet searches on companies and formatted proposals with e-mail follow-up, we need a renewed emphasis on face-to-face personal attention. Customers want to see their sales representative instead of hearing voice mail, and they want to know that if we promise something by a certain date, it will be fulfilled.

PAY ATTENTION TO DETAIL

Before I became a publisher of a Chicago real-estate publication, I began as a sales representative for a product with a poor sales record. I could not understand why anyone would refuse to buy an ad for a proven niche publication at a nominal cost. One day I started taking pictures of real estate with my camera, taught myself how to insert the photos into mock ads, and showed up at each customer's office with the ad and a photo of the building in it. This extra effort and personal touch differentiated me from the competition and contributed greatly to my success.

Above all, if I told a customer that I would do something, I would persevere until the task was complete. I hold myself to that standard today, both professionally and personally. Successful 21st Century Selling requires us to fight for our customer and cut through the "red tape" within our organizations in order to improve customer satisfaction. This effort solidifies customer loyalty and will be rewarded when budgets are cut and the business relationship continues.

I have noticed that the most popular books on sales techniques focus on what the authors refer to as SPIN training. Back when the anthologist of this book, Joe Cullinane, and I worked for Xerox in the '80s, SPIN was the hottest selling technique. It is all about customer relationship selling, asking probing questions, identifying the problem, presenting your product as a solution, and following up. Women have natural instincts to help accomplish that, but everyone should pay attention to incorporate the most important principle of personal and professional success in the selling strategy — building a relationship. It's a tenet, not a trend, that never goes out of style.

Sandra Swanson's 20-year career enabled her to build expertise in sales, marketing and training. She began as a systems analyst at Xerox Corporation and progressed over ten years to become the strategic accounts manager for the firm's technology division. She earned a "Top Sales Representative" award as well as participation in the Xerox President's Club.

She then became the publisher and sales manager for Relocation Consultants (RELCON) in Chicago, where she was a member of the Chicago Apartment Association and the Apartments Nationwide Board of Directors. Swanson successfully developed, implemented and managed corporate services and property-management sales campaigns, which involved database management, direct mail and an online newsletter.

After Swanson acquired RELCON, the *Chicago Tribune* quickly identified her sales ability and recruited her to be their Internet sales manager for the real estate, auto and employment classified advertising.

Swanson's reputation as a professional in the apartment industry earned her the position of vice president of sales for San Diego-based Spectrum Apartment Search. By instituting creative and well-planned marketing strategies within corporations and property-management companies, Swanson helped to promote this national company's growth. She also created and published comprehensive training materials for all levels of sales from field sales representatives to regional managers.

Contact:

Sandra Swanson

swan@san.rr.com

858-454-1051

CHAPTER ELEVEN

Execution: Aligning Around Your Differentiation

Your job, more than ever, is to help customers understand how they can most effectively get what they want by buying what you're selling.

By Dave Greene

Despite changes in the relentlessly competitive business environment of the new millennium, yesterday's 20th Century sales challenge and that of the 21st Century look fairly similar. Factors such as sales channels, major accounts, account management and various other strategies will continue to influence how we sell products and services.

Many facets of the sales business remain unchanged since they were first articulated by some of the early greats of the so-called modern era of selling, such as Dale Carnegie and W. Clement Stone. Although these earlier practitioners spoke more to the individual contributor and spent a great amount of time on attitude and interaction skills, it took the tremendous organizational selling machines of companies such as IBM and Xerox to institutionalize the science that selling has become. These sizable firms expanded strategies to include "consultative selling," "relationship selling," "solution selling" and many more well-conceived and successful methodologies for increasing sales efficiency and effectiveness.

This has led us all the way to the demanding frontiers of a new century that can only raise the bar on that most difficult and always-pressing question every sales organization must continuously answer: how is our product, service or organization clearly a better and different value?

Whether businesses will be selling to consumers or to other businesses, the answer to that question — the "value proposition" — will not be delivered through newer, better or more sophisticated technology. Nor will it be through customized marketing schemes designed to assure a customer's lifetime ownership. Ultimately, the answer will come from a very old-millennium resource called a sales force.

If this is true, then we can describe any uniquely 21st Century attribute as a "must have" in the never-ending arsenal of strategies, methodologies, techniques and formulas that always have been the staples of good sales management. What revolutionary change in the hallowed arena of selling befits the drama and symbolism of the 21st Century? I suggest it's nothing less than the ability to execute your value proposition to perfection.

Whatever your title, industry or the unique set of acronyms that represent the value of your product or service, you and your organization will still have to execute and deliver value on a personal level. Your customer has never been "a business" or "a consumer." Your customers have always been people who are trying to understand how they can more effectively get what they want by buying what you are selling – instead of what someone else is selling.

VIRTUAL VS. VALUE

Entering the new century, your customers are receiving more information more creatively packaged and rapidly delivered than ever before. The same ubiquitous technologies that have held the promise of "enabling" people to be more productive, more effective and more efficient also have had a disruptive effect on how we establish and communicate a differentiated value. The Internet – first ridiculously oversold as the framework for a new virtual economy and subsequently banished by the tribal council of investors for not producing ROI with the profits and predictability of the old economy – also has been guilty of permanently altering the traditional buy-sell equation.

As a conduit of information, the Internet easily has eclipsed every medium that has preceded it. More importantly, it has wrought the uneasy quality of being *interactive.* The marketing machinery responsible for the development and sale of brands has still not entirely absorbed the impact of this development, but it has and will continue to alter how the buyer relates to and does business with the seller. The traditional apparatus of marketing has been able to use highly effective television and print advertising to build brand recognition through a stream of one-way communications with the customer.

Sales messages and imagery have washed over the intended recipients who have passively absorbed the projected value proposition and, assuming things go according to plan, are dutifully drawn to the product or service preconditioned to buy. As any true marketing department will attest, the only obstacle to the sale is the sales force itself, the real selling having been accomplished by the marketing department and its compelling brand message.

Unfortunately for traditional marketers, technology has added an unforeseen twist with this new online medium. Now, customers actually want to have a *say* in how they will be sold. This clearly is going beyond the safe and controlled confines of a focus group. Here the customer wants to question, prod and practically dictate to the seller the look, shape and feel of the value proposition. Previously undisclosed performance gaps between the projected brand imagery and the actual brand experience are quickly seen in sharp contrast as buyer and seller engage in two-way communication that over time will determine the customer's true perception of the product's value. The marketing axiom that perception is reality has taken a nasty turn for some businesses as the consumer now tests for reality to ensure an accurate perceived value.

THE "EXPERIENCE" INITIATIVE

The automotive industry illustrates this latest sales challenge. In 2000, about 22,000 new vehicle dealers sold more than 17 million new vehicles worth $330 billion. The vast network of franchised new-vehicle dealers is the cornerstone of the vehicle manufacturers' retail-distribution system. It is a complex relationship between fiercely independent dealer entrepreneurs and highly structured and often bureaucratic manufacturing organizations. In the simplest terms, the manufacturer engineers, builds and sells the vehicle brand at a national level. The dealer in turn purchases inventories from the manufacturer, and markets and sells the vehicle to the local region while taking on the additional responsibility of ensuring customer service and satisfaction. The consumer automotive-value proposition is particularly difficult to execute, requiring both dealer and manufacturer to provide more service and better product for an increasingly difficult-to-attain profit margin.

With the exception of the occasional low-supply/high-demand vehicle line, product parity has never been more pronounced. Supplier costs have been reduced as much as possible, dealer margins have been reduced, and customer acquisition costs continue to increase. Since the early '70s, when Lee Iaccoca first popularized the customer incentive rebate, "Buy a car, get a check," manufacturers and their dealers have faced a steady commoditization of their product.

The manufacturer's search for differentiation has culminated in various initiatives targeted at creating a purchase and ownership "experience" uniquely suited to its brand identity. Yet, if you're General Motors (with more than 8,000 dealerships) or Ford Motor Company (with more than 5,000 dealerships), the potential exists for thousands of different "experiences," each dependent on the ability of the dealer to execute on a customer-acquisition strategy. In theory, if the "Subaru Difference" really is different at the point of dealer/consumer interaction, there will be a much higher probability that you'll be driving home a new Subaru than its nearest competitor. The strategy for customer acquisition will be communicated in every facet of the company's marketing plan. Most importantly, there will be an alignment of the projected brand "experience" with all customer interaction that occurs before the purchase decision and into the ownership cycle. This is one of the new realities of 21st Century Selling, and it isn't limited to the automotive industry.

Technology is forcing a slow, inexorable alignment of the seller's value promise and the customer's total value experience well beyond the question of price. If the one truth of the networked economy is that buyers now have massive quantities of information from which they are able to quickly make relevant buying decisions, eliminating value pretenders as they select value contenders, then flawless execution of a well-conceived value proposition is the new imperative.

INTEGRATED STRATEGY

Somewhere beyond the vernacular of the latest in marketing speak or catchy buzzwords intended to serve as shorthand for an implied strategy, a real sales force will learn winning depends on thoroughly executing a meaningful promise of customer value on a good product or service. This sales force will triumph over a competitor that hasn't made the commitment to consistent and flawless execution of strategy. The winning salesperson, the winning sales organization and the winning company will be in alignment with the particulars of that strategy from sales to finance to engineering. Traditional sales force "training" will not be limited to the sales force and methodologies. Rather, it will extend to the entire organization and include clear identification of the value proposition, the roles and responsibilities of each business unit to deliver on it, and the metrics that ensure everyone stays in alignment with agreed-upon objectives.

Training for these organizations will not be an exercise in abstract thought that somehow runs in parallel with the rest of the business and is limited to customer-contact personnel. Instead, what we commonly call "training" will be a carefully integrated strategy for customer acquisition and retention that is communicated throughout the organization. The sales force, in order to create and maintain a sustainable level of excellence in the execution of strategy, will actively manage the knowledge required to meet performance standards. A "learning partnership" will exist between the business units directly responsible for producing sales results and all other units responsible for supporting and maintaining results that will constantly exchange information that strengthens customer value both in product and delivery.

Arguably the best companies of the past — including Federal Express, IBM and Intel — have developed and implemented the ability to execute their value proposition as the ultimate differentiator. Certainly the concept is not new to the 21st Century. However, as we move ahead in this era of selling, it will be the new standard by which sales winners are differentiated from those whose "brand" has little resemblance to the customer's reality.

As the president of Automotive Learning Technologies, David Greene is involved in the design and development of training solutions for assisting OEM and dealer clients to effectively utilize new and emerging technologies in their retail growth strategies. Prior to founding this venture, Greene was vice president of sales and dealer network operations for Autoweb.com, one of the first publicly traded on-line auto buying services. He had overall responsibility for dealer sales, account management, dealer training and consulting services, and customer care.

Prior to joining Autoweb.com in 1998, Greene worked as a performance and training consultant with the Rikess Group, an automotive consulting group. There he worked with clients such as Ford Motor Company, AutoNation, Saab Cars USA, and Land Rover on issues including the design and development of dealer training for both national and international sales and management personnel. He has also been involved with developing sales and management procesess for some of the premier retail operations in the United States. He was an early advocate of customer-focused selling strategies and customer relationship management while running award-winning sales organizations for Lincoln-Mercury. Greene is also an active conference speaker and facilitator sharing his "real world" knowledge of dealers' best practices from across the country.

Contact:
David Greene
2299 Constitution Drive
San Jose, CA 95124
Office: (408) 269-7300
E-mail: david@automotivelearning.com

CHAPTER TWELVE

It's Time to Challenge the Idea That "Time Is Money"

In the 21st Century, relationships are money.

By Jeffrey Wildfogel, Ph.D.

Several years ago, I attended a free half-day sales seminar. You've probably been to one. They offer just enough information to convince you to lay out a large sum of money for a 40-hour course. This one, however, was one of the best I've attended because the presenter attempted to teach something of value rather than merely tell you the results you'd achieve if you anted up and enrolled.

The seminar attempted to teach 14 ways of asking open-ended questions — key qualities of peak performers in sales. But during role-playing exercises, everyone in the seminar had trouble asking more than a few open-ended questions. We kept returning to close-ended questions.

Why? By observing the role-plays and talking to the participants during the breaks, I realized their perspective — that "time is money" — made it difficult to ask open-ended questions. From this perspective, participants need to make assumptions concerning what people want and ask close-ended questions so that they can make the sale as quickly as possible. For example, they asked, "Do you want the refrigerator with the four-cubic-foot or the ten-cubic-foot freezer?" From their time-is-money perspective, an opened-ended question such as, "What would your dream refrigerator look like?" might lead to a long conversation that would be a waste of time — and money.

Is the time-is-money perspective bad? Only if you want to become a peak performer in sales. From my experience in making presentations at sales conferences, conducting sales workshops and coaching one-on-one, the salespeople in the seminar I attended were not unusual. It seems most salespeople have a time-is-money perspective. When you think that way, you may make the quick sale, but you won't have satisfied customers because your customers won't feel that they were truly heard or treated with respect.

There are three downsides to dissatisfied customers:

- The percentage of returns will be high because of buyer remorse. You convinced the customer to buy, but perhaps you were able to sell something he or she did not need or could not afford. Other misgivings will arise because your customer will feel ignored and therefore will not trust you or feel good about the sale even if it was what he or she really needed and could afford.

- Although you have made the sale, you have taken a small short-term gain at the expense of a larger long-term gain. In sales, the easiest sale to make is to a satisfied customer. If you make the sale but the customer is dissatisfied, next time he or she will look elsewhere. You lose the repeat business.

- Perhaps worst of all, when you make a sale to a less-than-satisfied customer, you have almost no chance of getting referrals. Sure, from a time-is-money perspective, you've made that one sale. But that's where it ends. You won't sell to the customer the second time, and you won't have access to friends and colleagues who might need your product. Ultimately, you've wasted a wonderful opportunity – the opportunity to turn one sale into three or even ten. Referrals, even more than repeat sales, are the lifeblood of a peak-performing salesperson.

What's more, when you make assumptions intended to close the sale as quickly as possible, you might assume incorrectly and thereby lose the original sale. Say you asked whether the customer wanted a four- or ten-page-per-minute printer. But what if speed was never an issue? By taking for granted that speed was the issue, perhaps because it is to most of your customers, you lost the opportunity to find out that this particular customer wanted reliability. Had you found that out, you would have known you had the ideal printer and made the sale — and had a satisfied customer. Too bad. You lose.

CHANGING PERSPECTIVES

If "time is money" is an ineffective perspective, what works better? In the seminar I spoke of earlier, I realized there was a better way to get salespeople to ask open-ended questions. Instead of seeing the world from the time-is-money viewpoint, you need to change your outlook to "relationships are money." In this latter perspective, you build your sales business by building quality relationships with your customers. Can you build these relationships by assuming what they want and asking close-ended questions that require "yes" or "no" or "this one" or "that one" answers? Of course not. You build a relationship by finding out what your clients' goals are, what they have tried to do to reach those goals, what has made it difficult for them to reach their goals, and what they believe they need to reach their goals.

You do that by asking open-ended questions. But it's no longer a technique. You don't need to keep telling yourself, "Now remember to ask open-ended questions, and remember there are the 14 ways to do it." Instead, by seeing the world from a *relationships*-are-money perspective, you will naturally want to get to know the person you are with and just as naturally begin to ask open-ended questions.

In the beginning of any good relationship, we want to get to know the other person, so we naturally ask open-ended questions. Think of a romantic relationship you've had. No one had to tell you to ask open-ended questions or teach you how to ask them. To start a conversation to help you get to know the other person, you ask "What do you like to do on the weekends?" and "What kind of movies do you like?" not "Do you like skiing?" and "Did you like *Sleepless in Seattle*?" Open-ended questions allow the person you want to know better to tell you more about himself or herself.

Techniques and tips rarely work because they are too hard to remember and too difficult to use when you're on the spot. Worse, even when you put them into action, they are often perceived for what they are — techniques — and are seen as insincere. I recall having a conversation with a salesperson who nodded and said "uh huh, right" every time I paused. It is, of course, important to let the person who is speaking know you're paying attention. And an effective way of building rapport is by nodding and saying "uh huh, right." As a technique, however, it doesn't work. The salesperson I was with made this same response every time I paused. Soon it became annoying. To test whether his responses were sincere or merely a technique, I began to pause at odd moments — even between syllables such as "sud (pause) denly." Every time I hesitated, he nodded and said "uh huh, right." The rest of us are not stupid. We know the difference between technique and sincerity. When we perceive someone is using a technique, the technique often has the opposite of its intended effect. I am not a violent person, but his "uh huh, right" responses were so annoying I was sorely tempted to pop him one in the nose.

From the relationship perspective, what would you want to know about your prospective customer? That is, to build a good relationship, what do you need to know? Here are some ideas and example questions from the clients I coach. After asking these questions, you will know enough about your prospective customers to know how to meet their needs.

- Issues/concerns in their company: What are the main concerns your company is having this year?

- What they have or are using now: What are you doing now to get people to know about your product?

- What they like most: What do you like most in the copiers you are using now?

- What they would change or improve: What would you like your telephone systems to do that they are not doing now?

- Personal goals and hot buttons: Imagine it is the end of the year. What is it that you have accomplished this year? What are you most proud of?

- Business goals in the company: Imagine it is a year from now and time for your annual review. What is it you want your manager to know you have accomplished?

- What has to be done right to achieve these goals: Imagine it is the end of the year and you have achieved your goals. What were the keys that enabled you to reach your goals?

- What things they would worry about most if something went wrong: What might prevent you from reaching your goals?

- How they would know when their goals have been successfully achieved: What are your criteria for determining whether your goals have been achieved?

- Information about who will use the product or service: Who will be using this product (service)? What are they looking for? I'd like to talk to them to find out their perspective on what they are looking for.

- Information about the buying decision: Who else is involved in the buying decision? What are they looking for? The last time this product (service) was bought, how was it determined to buy that particular product (service)? Has any thing changed in how buying decisions are made?

In our new-and-improved perspective, you not only want to get to know your prospective customers, but you also want them to get to know you. There's no opportunity for such dialogue when time is money. Rather, it's "get the sale as quickly as possible." But once again, you risk buyer's remorse, a high rate of returns, no repeat sales, no referral sales and maybe even no sale if the prospective client does not get to know you.

What do you want your prospective customer to know about you? You don't want to tell your prospective clients about your childhood, your parents and your difficulties in junior high school. Your time and theirs must be used wisely. In the "relationship" model, you want to let your prospective customer know what he or she needs to know to trust that you are looking out for his or her best interests; what you say about your product or service is true; and if there are problems in the future, you will be there to solve them. More simply, you want your customer to know you well enough to recognize that you are sincere, trustworthy and credible.

When I'm selling my services, I look for opportunities to tell my prospective customer my purpose and values. You, of course, will want to share your purpose and values. I want my prospective customers to know that I will help them develop mental skills and resources to enable them to become peak performers. I want them to know that if they are working with me, they can count on me to act as if I am on their team; that I will do all I can to ensure that everything I do for them makes a positive, powerful and long-lasting difference; that I will do my best for them at all times, without exception. I want to build a relationship of mutual understanding, respect and trust. And I can't do that unless I get to know them and they get to know me. I know that once I have built this relationship, I have a lifelong customer.

But, once again, be warned: if you tell your prospective clients about your purpose and values as a technique for building trust and getting lifelong sales, it will backfire. As a successful real estate agent client of mine said, "People can smell sincerity." If you communicate your values and purpose as a technique, you will be found out and your reputation ruined. Once your reputation is ruined, you can forget about sales as a career.

I communicate my purpose and values because that's who I am and how I want to run my business. Even if I could earn more money by making a quick sale, without regard to my client getting what he or she really needed, I wouldn't do it. Fortunately, it's not an either/or proposition. It's not either (1) come from a relationships-are-money perspective and be a good person or (2) make a ton of money. No, coming from a relationships-are-money perspective lets you be a good person **and** increases your chance of making money and reaching your other goals. But that only happens if you're genuine about it — not if it's merely a technique.

The salespeople in the seminar I attended were given 14 ways to ask open-ended questions but still asked close-ended questions in a sales role-play. Techniques alone are often not good enough to promote change. If I were teaching a seminar to get you to ask open-ended questions and more importantly, if I were teaching a seminar to give you the mental edge to become a peak performing salesperson, I'd help you change your perspective from "time is money" to "relationships are money."

Jeffrey Wildfogel's doctoral thesis in psychology from Stanford, a pioneer study in peak performance, explored performance under pressure. He has been a consulting professor of psychology at Stanford University for 18 years and currently teaches "The Psychology of Peak Performance," a class aired through the Stanford Center for Professional Development, as well as "The Mental Edge in

Sales," "The Art of Coaching in Business," "Challenging Assumptions and Creating Breakthroughs" and "The Psychology of Peak Performance for Groups."

Jeffrey is the founder and president of The Mental Edge, a consulting and training company that provides a broad range of tools for empowering people and organizations to meet the challenges of change and chaos. He has worked with both businesspeople and athletes. In the world of business, Jeffrey works primarily with executives, managers and salespeople, both in one-on-one achievement coaching sessions and group seminars. Jeffrey provides clients with the opportunity and mental technology to go beyond previous limits and invent their own paths to success. The result is breakthroughs in leadership, productivity and sales. His corporate clients include PC World, Hewlett Packard and Seville Properties.

Among his sports clients, he has consulted with the Stanford baseball and women's basketball teams, both of which won national championships. He also has been a personal achievement coach to Olympic, professional and All-America athletes.

He is the author of The Mental Edge in Sales: Authentic Selling®, a book that is due to be published later in 2002. Jeffrey also publishes a monthly e-newsletter, "The Mental Edge for Peak Performance."

Contact:
Jeffrey Wildfogel
The Mental Edge
201 San Antonio Circle, Suite 212
Mountain View, CA 94040
Phone: 650-948-9200
E-mail: jwildfogel@aol.com
Web site: www.thementaledge.com

It's Time to Challenge the Idea That "Time is Money"

CHAPTER THIRTEEN

Secrets of a Sales Interview

When pitching yourself for a new position,
there's a lot to learn from an inveterate recruiter.

By David Wolf

In the past 20 years, I've recruited and interviewed thousands of people for software sales in all of North America's major markets. We're talking about an exciting industry with strong financial compensation schemes — hence the keen competition for the prized positions.

How do you land one? The key to securing a job in the software sector, or any top-level sales job, is preparation. A lack of it is all too obvious when you're on my side of the desk. As a result, I'm offering perspective on what employers are seeking in 21st Century salespeople — and how prospective employees can meet their needs. For starters, you need to know who you are and what you bring to the table. Then you need to be able to paint a picture to the people who are conducting the interviews. In other words, you had better be ready.

PHONE FIRST

The first interview is usually done over the phone, and although no one can see you, it's important that you make your best impression. First, stand when you are talking on the phone. When you sit, your voice tends to get lower and energy gets trapped in your chest. Stand up. Walk around. You'll feel better and sound better.

Next, focus on the voice of the other person. The voice will tell you a lot if you listen carefully. The interviewer will get right to the issues, looking for keywords such as product categories or types of accounts and earnings history. You will need to help an interviewer see you for who you are. Your energy and your questions can lead to your strengths. Because the goal is to eliminate unwanted candidates, the interviewer will know within minutes whether to continue with you.

At the same time, you should be asking the same of yourself: Do *I* want to continue? Most recruiters don't really understand the value proposition of their companies. So cut them some slack on their knowledge base. Although a company will invest great resources to build a fabulous company, too often the staff will hire temporary recruiting help (read: minimum wage) to sell their story. The phone interviewers may have an excellent opportunity but not know how to express themselves — and you have just passed on the next Oracle or Siebel.

There are several goals for the first phone call. One is to look at the larger issues such as product space, the market and then the company. There will also be an intense look at the compensation plan. At one point, when the software market was exploding, the candidates had been hitting the first interview hard. Now that the pace has lessened, the process is more discerning. Software vendors learned that you had better hire people fast, or you might miss the market. So they couldn't ask too tough of a question, or they couldn't hit head-count goals.

As times have changed, the ten-minute phone interview has become more demanding. You need to use powerful picture words to describe yourself. You need to let them know of your sales skills and accomplishments. Let them know how you got where you are. Much of the in-depth information can't be nailed down during the phone screen interview. Besides, it would be wasting your ammo to give them both barrels too early. You need to feed the first screener enough data to reach the next level with the sales manager. Even the next interview, with the director or VP of sales, may be another short phone interview. If you pass these quickies, you earn the right to get grilled by the top executives in great detail — face to face.

TIME FOR NO. 2

Then again, it's not always face-to-face. In today's fast-paced world, with the eternal chasing of quarterly revenues, an in-person interview may be difficult to arrange when you and the sales manager are at opposite ends of the United States. This interview may still be remote by phone or video conferencing. If so, your energy level must be kept at a maximum. It is, of course, easier to do this in person. When we're in the same room, we learn to play off the other person's energy. When you're on the other end of a phone or a Kinko's video-conference setup, you have to manufacture your own energy. Candidates need to use powerful picture words to describe themselves.

Take the time I interviewed a woman I'll call Shelley. To start, Shelley described herself as passionate, articulate, intelligent, motivated and ambitious. She said she was taking sales classes — Solution Selling, for instance — at every opportunity to stay sharp. She attended seminars to keep up on technology trends. As a great networker, she kept up with old clients, even when they were no longer her accounts. She loved the challenge in developing new accounts. She was the sum total of aptitude, attitude and work habits. She got up early, worked out and then pounded the phones. Shelley said she led a balanced life and always ended up a top producer. When I heard this, questions about her product knowledge and other sup-posedly top criteria melted into the background.

Although the first interview is often a quick snapshot of the issues — essentially keyword conversations — this second one with the direct sales manager could end the process or lead farther down the road. How it works out rests with your resourcefulness and skills at selling yourself. Most experienced sales managers have preconceived ideas of what they are looking for. In the technology sector, whom you have worked for weighs almost as much as what you have done. But you need to take a good look at your career and realize what your strengths are. You also need to know what your weaknesses are. Then you need to be able to steer the conversation in the direction most beneficial to you. In the software industry, executives think product and client base first. Although I under-stand the importance of a quick start and content knowledge, there are more important things to consider.

We recently finished an assignment that illustrates my point — from the perspective of both interviewee and interviewer. After doing the initial phone interviews, in which we stayed close to the product content area and the compensation scheme, we winnowed the list down to eight candidates. The client, the director of sales, liked four of them. In the next step, we went back to the candidates and talked over the issues. Business development was paramount. The person for this job was going to need to be creative and disciplined in developing the accounts. The candidate we liked said, "I hate making cold calls! It's not me. In my entire career I've always walked into situations where I took an installed base and hit home runs." So much for that candidate. The interviewee missed an opportunity to put a positive spin on his talents.

The three final candidates were as follows. One had a tier-one pedigree. He was a BSEE and then worked for all tier-one vendors. He was what I call an emerging "A" player. He hadn't hit the cover off of the ball, but you could tell he was on the way. The other two candidates were both at the top of their game. They produced excellent numbers for their companies and were making great money. The manager went with the pedigree. He felt his VP of sales in California would buy the pedigree easier. This was their first time working together at this company, and he wanted his first hire to be a no-brainer. The other two candidates were stronger, but the manager had other priorities. Lesson No. 1: what you think are the criteria might be sidetracked by a political agenda. This is why candidates and clients need a strong pipeline on both ends.

If anything, this story underscores the point of being prepared. Take stock of what you really have to offer. Then be ready to give an executive your elevator pitch about yourself.

MULTIPLE INTERVIEWS AND BEYOND

Expect multiple interviews if you are being evaluated for a position with the executive management team. This is true in the case of higher sales- and marketing-management executives. They need to meet the COO, the CEO, the CFO, product-development people and possibly board members. You can imagine by their titles that they are going to have different concerns. You need to pay attention to their position and what they need to hear.

Example: we placed a senior salesperson who was selling about $7 million a year. He got caught up in a RIF from a major supply-chain firm and we were sending him to a simple but very effective e-procurement engine play. He knew the territory and the application content cold. The executive management team was thrilled with this person, and he liked them. When he made his trip to corporate headquarters, he told the product-development people he could sell this without even a demo. He totally understood the value proposition, and he knew how the customers would respond. Well, they were aghast. How could someone buy their baby without looking at it or trying it on? The team panned this person's candidacy.

We made it through that issue, however, and he started. Within three weeks, he closed his first deal for nearly $900,000. Meanwhile, he made major contributions in pricing and contract changes that will take this vendor forward years in advance. But he almost blew it. When you are in front of the product-development people and are admiring their baby, it helps to appreciate their work.

At the same time, you need to be true to yourself. While you are selling yourself to interviewers, you are gathering information that will help you decide whether the company is right for you. You don't want to accept a position that is built for failure. If the firm needs someone who is great at business development, and you aren't, then it won't work. If the opening is for someone who can close a lot of small deals or a lot of big deals, and that's not you, it won't work. If you are a sales manager who hasn't done a lot of recruiting, you're going to have a learning curve.

The bottom line: don't set yourself up for failure. Many candidates tell us, "I'm a great relationship-type salesperson." Relationships are fine, but first go find a new account and sell them – then you can tell me about relationships. When the market is on fire, we have to hire basically anyone who has a breath. When things are getting tight, it's a different story. Software vendors are cutting the fat while trying to build muscle. The muscle is stronger, better, tougher, more accountable sales management and sales teams. Too many software vendors have 25 percent of the sales team selling all their product. The other 75 percent sell nothing. Amazing.

People on both sides of the fence are not doing their jobs during the interviewing process. We all need to take a hard look at the criteria being set up. Do we need people like the passionate and articulate woman I talked about? Or do we need people who understand technology content? I suggest we need a combination of both features.

WHAT ARE YOU MADE OF?

For your part, look at yourself. Be critical but not overly so. Understand your personal skills. Put your house in order. Learn that you have certain technology content, self-imposed or not. Be ready — ready to discuss products, competitors, pricing, sale cycles, sale methodologies, accounts, business development techniques, base salaries, draws, quotas and performance. Be ready to talk about where you have been most successful and why. This time of self-evaluation is a good time to embark upon some improvement processes. If you have stopped learning, you're done. I see legions of listless middle-career executives. I start yawning as they tell me how great they were a couple of years ago and they just haven't got traction lately. Sorry. Next!

Remember, long-term jobs are a thing of the past. We are all temps, whether we realize it or not. The average life of a VP of sales is 18 months. So you can imagine what the field organization looks like. Our world changes so fast that those who are not striving to be better by default must fall behind. You have to be ready to interview and make your case about every two years. It once was three-and-a-half years, but that, too, has changed.

Successful people have pride in themselves. Their pride won't let half-measures be their destiny. Live every day with passion and focus and discipline, and the results will follow. You will always be ready for an interview. The answers to appropriate questions will flow out of you, and the other side will recognize you as a player. Ultimately, you'll land the job, and the company will be pleased with your results. In other words, both sides win — the best possible scenario in any sales sector. And, in a way, it's all because of you. As for clients, please think about this. Even now in this period known as the post dot.bomb era, there are still not enough "A" players to go around.

For the past 25 years, David Wolf has been helping software vendors build their North American sales teams. Although most of his clients are based on the coasts, with a focus on Silicon Valley, Huntersoft is located in the Midwest, which is home to one-third of the clients for whom Wolf has been helping build leading sales teams. Huntersoft has a half-dozen recruiters and more than 1,200 software vendors in its database.

Off the job, Wolf has been studying martial arts for most of his adult life, and he keeps his edge – literally – with his study of WingChun Kung Fu and Kali, which is a Filipino stick and short sword fighting martial art. Wolf, who has been married for 15 years and has one son named Spencer, lives on Lake Shore Drive in Chicago and looks forward to many more years in the software marketplace.

Contact:

David Wolf

Huntersoft

Phone: 312-944-7563

E-mail: david@huntersoft.com

CHAPTER FOURTEEN

The Essence and Elements of 21st Century Selling

It's an Evolution, NOT a Revolution

By Joe Cullinane

In answering the question — "What is 21st Century Selling?" — we should acknowledge what it is not.

- It is not a substitute for hard work and smart thinking.
- It is not a panacea or a silver bullet for success.
- It is not a revolution.

21st Century Selling is, however, an evolution that combines the best of traditional selling with the new tools available through information technology to create a new model of selling. Companies such as Cisco, Intel and Dell have been selling billions of dollars of products and services over the Internet. We are not just talking about selling books - these companies and many others sell complex, high-ticket items on the Web.

21st Century Selling is a high-touch, high-tech approach to selling. It is a common-sense approach that uses easy-to-implement, low-cost tools and tested methods. In these days of difficult travel, 21st Century Selling offers a way to minimize travel and maximize customer contact.

Figure 1: The 21st Century Selling "sweet spot"

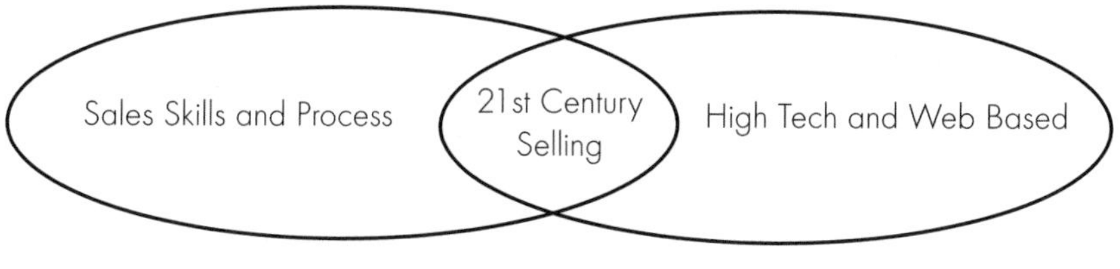

Sales Skills and Process · 21st Century Selling · High Tech and Web Based

TRADITIONAL SELLING VS. INTERNET SELLING

Traditional selling methods have evolved during the past half-century and were originally developed by companies such as IBM and Xerox. Traditional selling includes areas such as sales skills, presentation skills, account management, sales management and other skills and processes that have been refined to a high level of effectiveness. There are however, some drawbacks to traditional selling, including long and expensive sell cycles, the requirement for many face-to-face meetings, extensive travel and skepticism among prospects toward over-used methods.

With the advent of the PC, the Internet and wireless communication, the focus shifted to using technology for selling. Companies jumped into self-service Web sites, e-commerce, auctions and exchanges to sell their products. In fact, many sales tasks and processes can be done online. We can contact, survey, qualify, present, propose and close online. Some believed that the Internet would make traditional selling obsolete.

But the Internet is not a self-contained solution. It cannot do all the selling by itself. Technologists have been trying to build human intelligence in computer technology for a generation. But they have not been able to build in the subtlety of human communication, which is the essence of selling. Computers can't detect the hesitation in a voice that signals a lack of understanding or know when an objection has been posed. Technology simply cannot provide the same levels of service as a professional salesperson.

So as the new century began, we were left with an apparent Hobson's choice between traditional sales approaches considered obsolete and high-tech selling that over-promised and under-delivered.

It turns out those aren't the only two choices. The third - and we would suggest correct - choice is the evolutionary, blended approach that 21st Century Selling offers, combining the best of both worlds.

Figure 2: Using Internet technology and traditional methods creates a high-touch, high-speed method of selling.

21ST CENTURY SELLING APPROACH

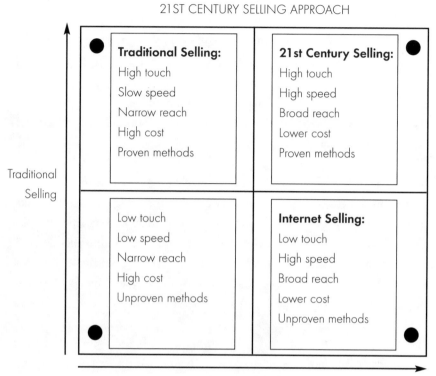

Application of Technology

Below are some important benefits of 21st Century Selling:

- Reduced travel requirements and costs
- Increased sales productivity and effectiveness
- Increased group participation
- Global reach
- 24-by-7 selling
- Shortened and compressed sales cycles
- Increased customer contacts and sales presentations
- A greater connection to prospects and customers
- Easy access to customer and competitive and information.

SEVEN STEPS TO 21ST CENTURY SELLING

Below are some of the elements of 21st Century Selling. These are easy, low-cost, fast ways to get started.

1. DEFINE AND STREAMLINE YOUR SALES PROCESS

Every product or service has a sales process, defined or not. The first step is to understand and document it. Once we have defined the process, we can then streamline and automate it. I have helped numerous companies streamline their sales process using the Internet. I call this process ECAP - electronic customer acquisition process.

Some examples of ECAP include streamlining and automating lead responses with customized introductory e-mails, and using online newsletters to help you stay in front of prospects. (See Attraction/Magnetic model.) Other ECAP tools include Web-based presentations, online demos and webinars that save time and money, reduce travel time and increase customer contact. It is important to note the sales process must account for the steps buyers must take to procure products and services.

TIPS
- You must first understand your sales process before automating it.
- Involve the salesperson in every part of the process.
- Have online versions as well as hard copies of your marketing materials to provide prospects. (Some people are still not online or prefer traditional materials. We all process information differently, so let prospects have what they want.)
- Use tools such as Webex for remote presentations and demos.
- Try a remote online seminar.
- Work with professionals who understand the sales process and the use of technology.

2. CREATE AN ATTRACTION/MAGNETIC SALES MODEL

An attraction or magnetic model is designed to draw prospects to your sales universe by offering something of value in return for their attention. The most commonly used tool for this model is the e-newsletter that it is delivered via e-mail. By the way, e-mail is the Internet's most widely used business application. It's a great relationship-building tool, providing an easy and effective way to contact and keep in touch with prospects and customers.

E-mail can help you stay fresh in your prospect's mind by letting you share valuable information on a regular basis.

TIPS

- Ask permission and allow your customers to opt in and out.
- Provide valuable information, not just sales material. Make the newsletter something prospects look forward to receiving and are willing to pass on (viral marketing).
- Make sure it is professional and consistent.
- Sign up for other online newsletters to get ideas for yours.
- Do not send "spam" e-mail messages.

3. USE E-LEARNING AND RESEARCH

The Internet provides a low-cost way to train geographically dispersed salespeople. It is also a great source of knowledge for individuals. Webinars, expert coaches, white papers, e-magazines and industry newsletters let you stay current. Many companies are also sponsoring information sessions over the Internet. It is getting much more expensive to have salespeople attend traditional training. The Web is a great alternative. It's much easier to log on and learn.

The Internet is also the best sales research tool ever invented. You can learn everything about competition and your prospects, particularly if they are public companies. Financial performance, business plans, key customers, key executive profiles and company mission statements are usually available on companies' Web sites. Use the Internet to keep your sales force well trained and well informed.

TIPS

- Visit your prospects' sites to learn about their objectives and about the customers they serve.
- Visit the Web sites of research companies such as IDC, Gartner, Jupiter and Forrester. They often provide great information for free.
- Edgar online, Bloomberg and other financial services firms are also great sources of financial information.
- Sites such as CEOexpress.com act as clearinghouses for many business and news sites.

- Determine how your company can use the Internet to train your people, and give it a try.
- See what online courses and webinars are available in your area of interest.

4. USE ONLINE COLLABORATION TO CONNECT

Internet technology provides an unprecedented opportunity to connect companies with their customers, linking sales and support teams across geographic locations worldwide. Sales executives, sales management, sales support, salespeople, partners, prospects and customers have a new opportunity to connect and collaborate.

The activities that are best suited to collaboration include:
- Account reviews
- Coaching sessions
- Brainstorming and strategy sessions
- Sales meetings
- Product and sales training
- Presentations
- Implementation strategies

TIPS

- Research the best tools for collaboration including chat rooms, message boards, quick messaging, Web video conferencing, online white boards, etc.
- Determine the best processes and meetings to conduct online.
- Connect with your audience.
- Make your interaction relevant and professional.
- See what your competitors and customers and using for collaboration.

5. CREATE 21ST CENTURY PARTNERSHIPS AND ALLIANCES

According to Jordan Lewis, author of *Partnerships for Profit*, "Strategic alliances provide access to far more resources than any single firm owns or could buy." This is even truer in the Internet age when a company can get tremendous leverage by working with partners. Many of your partners will promote your site or company if they believe it will benefit their customers or lead to revenue generation. You can also gain access to your partners' clients to sell your products. Strong partnerships can result in increased revenue, more prospects and greater customer satisfaction.

6. SALES ENABLE YOUR WEB SITE

Your Web site can become a powerful tool for selling. This approach involves using your Web site as a presentation tool, through which both parties view the same Web pages at the same time. You can interactively direct your prospects to presentations, case studies, surveys, success stories and product demos. This can be done using co-navigation tools or simply the telephone to guide their attention. In contrast to self-directed Web sites, you can work directly with prospects, answering objections and questions immediately. This is a low-cost, fast way to upgrade the effectiveness of your Web site.

7. UNDERSTAND THE POWER OF 21ST CENTURY CONVERGENCE

21st Century Selling is about the convergence of traditional selling and technology. It also involves using your existing intellectual property (IP) and materials in exciting new ways. The concept is to look for ways to translate and transfer intellectual property, products and marketing information, and maximize their value. Some examples include transforming an existing seminar or class into a webinar or online training. A methodology or white paper can be expanded to become a book, which can then become an e-book. Your IP can be combined to create new packages of products and services. A book, a CDROM, a Web site, Web-based presentations, downloadable white papers, handbooks and audiocassettes all can transform your existing IP into new product packages. By combining physical and online IP assets, you can create powerful new 21st Century tools for selling.

TIPS

- Review your intellectual property, and look for new ways of using what you have.
- Learn as much as you can about the convergence of technology. This is the biggest trend of the next five years.
- Combine physical intellectual property with digital products to create packages of IP that bring new and greater value to your customers.
- Explore how you can combine your IP with your partners' to create new products and approaches.
- When designing any material, training or methodology, keep convergence in mind.

JOIN THE FOREFRONT OF 21ST CENTURY SELLING

We have only touched a small portion of 21st Century Selling. There are many technologies and methods that apply. Technologies such as Web, video and audio conferencing, chat rooms, webcasts, portal technologies, streaming media, online storage of presentations, groupware and others all can be used to help increase sales efficiency and effectiveness.

In his book *Cyber Rules*, Tom Siebel, founder of Siebel Systems, writes, "Going digital isn't a hurdle for you to overcome; it is a once-in-a-millennium chance to seize the economic high ground."

In 21st Century Selling, you still need proven sales skills, knowledge and methods. But only when you learn to combine those traditional sales assets with the power of the Internet and other technology-based sales assets will you join the forefront of 21st Century Selling professionals.

Joe Cullinane is a sales and marketing consultant, coach and author. Joe also teaches graduate-level marketing classes.

Joe has held various executive positions with Diversified Software Systems, Inc., a leading enterprise software company, including vice president of strategic business development, vice president of marketing and vice president of international sales. Earlier, he held executive and sales positions with SalesLink Systems, Xerox Corporation and NCR Corporation.

Joe holds a master of science in communication degree from Northwestern University, a master of business administration degree from Dominican University, and a bachelor of science degree in marketing from Northern Illinois University. He has published several articles and appeared on business radio. Joe lives with his wife and son in Saratoga, California.

Contact Info:
joecullinane@hotmail.com
408-867-1663

Concluding Thoughts on 21st Century Selling

If you're reading this book, you're probably in sales or sales management, or at least are interested in selling. But you have other roles in your life, too – sometimes as a <u>buyer</u>. Your experiences as a buyer provide an important context for evaluating your knowledge, skills and expectations as a seller. A major recurring focus of this book is the importance of understanding and satisfying the buyer (even, as in Chapter 13, when the "product" you're selling is <u>yourself!</u>)

In the preceding chapters, we've explored the world of selling and discovered that it has many facets – understanding the buying cycle, using planning teams, partnering wisely, marketing to niches, using technology-based tools and systems such as e-mail and SFA, understanding the process and costs of acquiring customers, and the overriding importance of creating, building and sustaining relationships with your customers.

The concept for the book was to bring together top sales leaders with different experience and backgrounds, and present their prescriptions for and perspectives on sales success. Although in some areas the authors' views differ, it is surprising how much they have in common.

So what have we learned from this book? And what are some of the common elements?

- A focus on the buyer is the top priority.
- Technology is an important tool for sales success but not the be-all-end-all.

- Process is important, but you must always keep the buyer in mind.
- We must challenge our old assumptions about selling.
- Tools and methods of selling are different in the 21st Century, but the fundamentals are the same: know your product and how it benefits your customers.

We hope you have learned a few new ideas or concepts that will challenge your assumptions and enhance your abilities as a sales professional.

Welcome to a powerful new world of selling. Welcome aboard the ride of your life – the 21st Century Unlimited. It's a trip that has just begun. And its destination is up to you.

Joe Cullinane